The
—— Slim Palate ——
Paleo Cookbook

written and photographed by

Joshua Weissman

Victory Belt Publishing Inc.
Las Vegas

First Published in 2014 by Victory Belt Publishing, Inc.

ISBN-13: 978-1-628600-11-7

Printed in the USA

RRD 0114

contents

introduction

As a little boy I loved to cook. I would stand at the ready in the bustling kitchen, helping with every task I could as my anticipation for the meticulously prepared feast swelled. There are even photos of a 4-year-old me with a chef's hat the size of my torso towering over my head.

Unfortunately, as I got older, I drifted away from these practices to try other things, and I fell into a pattern of unintentionally poor eating that caused me to slowly gain weight and become obese. School grew difficult for me due to extreme ridicule and physical harassment from other students. I began to realize how much being overweight plagued me daily and was causing me to be increasingly unhappy. From age 9 to 14 I lived through this torment until, at the age of 15, I decided to change everything. I completely transposed my eating habits almost overnight and began eating real foods with consideration rather than labeled "diet" foods. Slightly more than a year and a half passed, and I lost over 100 pounds (before and after picture on page 258).

This journey rekindled the love for cooking that I'd had as a child. Back in the kitchen, I took it a step further and started my food blog, Slim Palate, which flourished thanks to the kind and generous real-food community. Eventually it led to this cookbook that you hold in your hands, a cookbook in which I can share my recipes and my story in a way that I hope everyone can enjoy and learn from.

In America and some other places (but not many, to be honest), people have a massive disconnect with food. This void—a void that I fell into myself—seems to be swelling at a rapid rate. Without realizing it, people have turned away from real, whole foods like meats, vegetables, and fruits in favor of packaged foods that are dense with processed carbohydrates and sugar. These foods line supermarket shelves, with labeling gimmicks designed to make people think that they are healthy choices. The average person is much more likely to pick up a box of Wheat Thins than a zucchini in an attempt to live healthier, which to me is rather baffling.

The biggest mistake I have ever made was to disconnect with real food. Because reconnecting was such a key component of my journey, I want to help others reconnect, whether you want to know more about your food, become healthier, or lose weight.

If losing weight is your goal, then I need to set one thing straight right off the bat: Losing weight is not easy, especially as you get closer to your goal. And the more weight you want to lose, the harder it gets. That doesn't mean you should fear stepping up and trying to make a change, though. I promise you that I didn't get it right the first time, or even the first few times. Take it head on, and let good nutrition be your pencil and time be your eraser.

frameworks to reconnect with food

My goal in writing this book is not to tell you how to eat, start a new way of eating, or launch some "celebrity diet." However, I do believe that there are certain places people should begin in order to learn how to listen to their bodies and reconnect with food. It doesn't come naturally to some people, myself included, so it is helpful to have a framework—more specifically, to have guidelines so that you can learn which foods make you feel good and perform well. The Weston A. Price Foundation and Paleo/primal ways of eating are great places to start and learn—or even to remain for a lifetime.

Weston A. Price Foundation

Weston A. Price, sometimes called the Isaac Newton of nutrition, was a dentist. In the late 19th century, he began studying the relationship between diet and dental health. By the 1930s, his research had led him to conclude that real, whole foods, including the fat-soluble vitamins found exclusively in animal fats, contribute to both dental and overall health. The organization that bears his name promotes eating nutrient-dense whole foods such as organically grown produce, grass-fed and pastured meats, and raw grass-fed dairy. To learn more about the Weston A. Price Foundation, visit westonaprice.org.

Paleo/Primal

This way of eating is similar to the Weston A. Price Foundation's but eliminates grains, legumes, and in some cases dairy. Paleo promotes the idea that we should be eating what the human body was designed to eat based on what humans have been eating for thousands of years. People who follow a Paleo/primal diet avoid foods that were unavailable in the Paleolithic era, prior to the advent of agriculture and the cultivation of grains. This means no bread, no oatmeal, no quinoa, no beans; just real, whole, nutrient-dense vegetables, fruits, meats, nuts, and seeds. Many people boast of the health benefits of eating Paleo, from enhanced workout performance to simply feeling amazing every day. If you would like to learn more about Paleo, there are many excellent websites devoted to it, including robbwolf.com, marksdailyapple.com, and chriskresser.com.

No matter how you choose to eat, the most important thing is to eat real, whole foods and find what makes you feel your best. During a lot of my weight loss, I followed the Weston A. Price guidelines, but I switched to a Paleo way of eating about three-fifths of the way through my journey, which made a significant difference in my physique and overall wellness. After eating Paleo for a while, I began experimenting with some of the foods I had eliminated to see what my body could and couldn't tolerate. I have found a way of eating that works for me that I continue to explore and expand.

eat fat fearlessly

One of the keys to my losing weight and becoming healthier was abandoning my fear of fat. I can understand if it takes someone a bit of time to get used to the notion of not fearing fat, because I had an incredibly difficult time believing it, too. I avoided fat like the plague—especially after being told my whole life that fat is bad for you. Health "experts" suggest that if you eat fat (especially saturated fat), you will get fat and develop heart disease. But what if I told you that much of what you have been told about fat is wrong?

If you look at human history, levels of heart disease and obesity began increasing dramatically only when refined carbohydrates and refined sugars began showing up in foods and on store shelves everywhere. Natural animal fats began being vilified in 1961 when *Time* magazine published an article based on the work of physiologist Ancel Keys and his now-famous *Seven Countries Study*. Keys analyzed participants from more than twenty-two countries for correlations between saturated fat consumption and heart disease, yet he included only seven of those countries in his graph. Including only seven out of twenty-two countries made his hypothesis appear correct, so his study was published. If he had included the other fifteen countries, no correlation would have been proven. Keys' study—a combination of biased and bad science—essentially started the whirlwind of saturated fat demonization.

In the real-food community, which includes the Weston A. Price Foundation and Paleo, Keys' study has been well discredited. A growing number of health practitioners are expressing disbelief in Keys' study and are trying to bring opposing viewpoints into the mainstream, but to little avail—at least so far. The fact that saturated fat makes up a significant portion of our cell membrane structure should be a trigger to take a step back and consider that saturated fat is something we may not want to eliminate from our diet. Not to mention that some of the supplements recommended by so-called "health experts" contain essential fat-soluble vitamins such as A, D, and K2 that are found in high concentrations in saturated fats like grass-fed tallow and butter. While it's fairly obvious that I am not opposed to the consumption of saturated fat, I'm just pointing out

another reason that the crusade against saturated fat and especially animal fat seems misguided and not very well thought out in many cases.

One of the reasons this notion goes unchallenged by the mainstream "health industry" is that saturated fat contains cholesterol, a natural substance that our bodies happen to produce. The argument is that the consumption of saturated fat increases cholesterol levels, and high cholesterol leads to heart disease. Well, it's true that saturated fat consumption can increase cholesterol, but it increases *total* cholesterol. Yes, LDL (bad cholesterol) goes up, but so does HDL (good cholesterol). Many studies show no correlation between total cholesterol and heart disease. In other words, there is no evidence that the consumption of saturated fat and cholesterol-rich foods increases heart disease risk. In fact, if you look at the course of America's health, the rate of heart disease has risen dramatically since Americans began severely limiting saturated fat. Compare that to countries like France and Spain, where rates of heart disease are low, while saturated fat intake is far from limited. In countries where people eat a lot of animal products and/or saturated fat and do have higher risks of heart disease, there are other contributing factors that could lead to heart disease.

Nowadays, the general consensus on fat is moving in a more positive direction; doctors and the FDA are talking about the good fat in foods like avocados, nuts, and olive oil, also known as monounsaturated fat, having positive effects on heart function and weight stability. But they still leave out saturated fat.

I'm making a point of this because as soon as you start incorporating healthy fats like avocados, nuts, olive oil, and yes, even animal fats, the easier time you will have feeling full and satisfied without overeating. Eating real food without fear frees you from feeling hungry all the time, while you burn fat or just feel healthier. So rejoice, and enjoy cooking with tallow, lard, butter, and whatever other animal fats you please. Take pride in that satisfying bite of fatty and juicy rib-eye or crispy-skinned chicken thigh, because life isn't about eating nothing but broiled chicken breasts and steamed broccoli.

Now, despite what I've said, I am not advising you to eat unlimited amounts of fat. There is such a thing as too much; it's just incredibly difficult to eat too much fat if you're eating properly already. Unless you're downing quarts of melted lard all day long (which I don't think is even possible), I'm not worried about your fat intake. Use your satiety and common sense as a guide, because everyone is different in terms of what they should consume. If my explanation is not thorough enough for you, I highly recommend reading up about saturated fat and cholesterol on websites like westonaprice.org, chriskresser.com, and marksdailyapple.com, all of which provide substantial amounts of sound information regarding this debate.

the calories in, calories out myth

Letting go of calorie counting was another key to my weight loss success. The prevailing notion is that as long as you are expending the same number of calories that you eat in a day, you won't gain weight. This hypothesis may seem legitimate (it has a bit of truth to it, but only in certain situations), but it's far from correct in my experience. What is really important is a system of hormones that decide whether it is okay to release fat. One of those hormones is insulin, which is produced in the pancreas and controls glucose metabolism and absorption by cells.

Now, insulin isn't a bad guy; in fact, we need it to live. In a physically fit person, insulin drives nutrients into the muscles, also known as glycogen stores. Glycogen stores are depleted through physical activity, like a workout. After you work out and deplete your glycogen stores, your body can deal with an insulin spike and utilize that insulin to drive those nutrients into your muscles. Insulin typically spikes when you eat foods that are higher in carbohydrates or sugar. Because so many people who are overweight eat a diet high in carbohydrates and sugars, their insulin levels are probably chronically high. And because they are also not as physically active as they should be to match a diet so rich in carbohydrates and sugar, their glycogen stores are probably already full when they eat a carb- and sugar-rich meal. The problem is that once the glycogen stores in your muscles and liver are full, you end up with excess glucose (sugar) in your system, and your body must find a place to put it—most commonly in fat cells and stored as triglycerides. In simpler terms, excess glucose in the body causes fat to be stored because insulin can't find anywhere else to put it to use in the body.

That said, the body metabolizes complex carbohydrates much more slowly than simple carbohydrates like table sugar, fruit sugar (fructose), and honey. Simple carbohydrates (sugars) are put into glycogen stores immediately. Sugars can quickly fill up liver glycogen stores, leaving the muscles empty and allowing excess glucose to raise blood sugar levels. So if you eat lots of simple carbohydrates (sugars), you're going to hit your storage limit much faster than you would with complex carbohydrates. In other words, if you were to prioritize the consumption of these two things, you would want to limit sugar much more heavily.

This is why the calories in, calories out hypothesis is rather ridiculous: it implies that you could essentially eat your day's worth of calories with the bulk of them coming from carbohydrates, both simple and complex, and not suffer any negative effects. Now, this might be possible in a physically fit person who is very active and is putting that insulin production to use through depleted muscle glycogen stores, but what about a person who isn't physically active? Despite the fact that this person *may* be eating within his "proper" caloric boundaries, he could easily be spiking his blood sugar far too much for his activity level, which forces his body to turn excess glucose into body fat. But what if you're working out *and* eating within your proper caloric boundaries, albeit with a high ratio of carbohydrates? Here's the thing: Your body will make every effort to burn off the sugary food you're eating before it bothers dipping into stored fats for energy. This means that, while your blood sugar levels might be more stable than those of an inactive person eating a similar sugar-rich diet, it's likely that you still won't be burning fat or losing any weight. This is a situation that a lot of people find themselves in, thinking that they can simply work off everything they eat, which isn't always the case.

I wanted to keep this discussion short and to the point to avoid overwhelming anyone with the science, but if you'd like to learn more, there are sources out there that explain how this works in great detail, such as the book *Why We Get Fat* by Gary Taubes and websites like marksdailyapple.com and chriskresser.com.

carbohydrate consumption for those who actually want to lose weight

People tend to be very interested in exactly how I ate during my 100-pound weight loss because it worked so well for me, but I can't sit down and explain it to every person who asks. My goal isn't to make this a diet or weight loss book, but I do want to take a moment to help those who wish to lose weight by sharing what I know and what has worked for me. Just be aware that this section isn't targeted to you unless your objective is to lose weight.

While I strongly support eating real food for general health, it isn't that simple when it comes to losing weight. Yes, real food needs to be the focus of your diet, but the assumption that *all* real food will help you lose weight overlooks a couple of specifics. Just because it's real food and not processed doesn't mean that it will help you lose weight, even though it may keep you healthy. This is the problem I experienced before I started regulating my carbohydrate and sugar consumption and was just counting calories and fat grams: I wasn't gaining weight, but I wasn't losing any, either.

For example, because I thought it was healthy, I had a medium smoothie from a local smoothie joint every day after my workout. Now, the smoothies I was consuming did fit into the calorie count I had set for myself, but each one also contained well over 80 grams of sugar and 100 grams of carbohydrates. Obviously, the sugar and carbohydrates were impeding everything. Believe it or not, even the natural carbohydrates and sugar in fruit are a problem for an overweight person when it comes to fat loss. Sugar of any kind in abundance, even if it's raw honey, organic fruit, or organic cane sugar, can keep your blood glucose level too high, thus causing your body to store fat rather than burn it. The second I learned that, I started moderating my carbohydrate and sugar intake and began integrating more healthful fats like avocados, nuts, extra-virgin olive oil, and animal fats into my diet, and I noticed real progress. By reducing and moderating your carbohydrate and sugar intake, you can lower those insulin spikes, leaving your body room to burn fat rather than hold onto it. This is exactly why low-fat diet meals that are full of carbohydrates and sugars rarely help you lose weight. I tried all those diet meals, and none of them worked for me.

After studying several books and articles, I found *The Belly Fat Cure* by Jorge Cruise to be the most useful to me. From a weight loss perspective, I highly recommend this book for anyone who is new to this. If you know nothing about Weston A Price or Paleo, start here, and then, if you so choose, move toward Weston A. Price or Paleo way of eating. Through my own experimentations and by utilizing methods from this book, I devised daily carbohydrate and sugar limits for myself. While I don't agree with all of Jorge's methods, he has an incredibly well-designed plan for carbohydrate and sugar consumption if you aren't ready to try anything very-low-carbohydrate (although I do recommend that you try going progressively lower-carbohydrate and see how it goes). I tried to eat only 110–120 grams of carbohydrates and 14–16 grams of sugar per day, including the sugars and carbohydrates in fruits and vegetables. In fact, I avoided fruits like bananas and apples entirely and stuck to blackberries, raspberries, and blueberries, which are significantly lower in sugar and carbohydrates. I tracked carbohydrates and sugars simply by adding them up throughout the day. To keep the math from being too much of a hassle, I tried to make sure that I ate no more than 40 grams of carbs and no more than 5 grams of sugar per meal.

You can certainly go *lower* than 110–120 grams of carbs and 14–16 grams of sugar a day; those numbers are limits, not goals. Don't strive to eat 40 grams of carbs or 5 grams of sugar at every meal, either; just be sure not to go above those limits if you're trying to lose weight. In fact, you could go even lower to something like 30–50 grams of carbs a day; that level may even be ideal for some people.

Granted, counting is really necessary only for those who are not going Paleo. If you try the Paleo way of eating, you will be much less likely to overeat carbohydrates or sugars. It's still possible to do it unconsciously, though, if you eat too many high-sugar fruits or starchy vegetables. Just be sure you know which foods are high in carbohydrates and sugars, and minimize your consumption of those foods.

Always read labels and look for added sugars, additives, and preservatives among the ingredients. Just because something is Paleo does not mean that it will help you lose weight or burn fat—just look at those "Paleo" treats that pack 10–30 grams of sugar into a small single serving. When I pick up something that has a nutrition label on it, the first three things I look at are the ingredients and then the carbohydrate and sugar numbers. You can use websites like calorieking.com (for the macronutrient profiles, not necessarily the calorie counts) and nutritiondata.self.com to find the sugar and carbohydrate counts for practically any fruit or vegetable, seeing as most whole fruits and vegetables do not have a nutrition label. If you don't know the serving size for something, a good general rule is that a serving of fruit or higher-sugar vegetable (like beets or carrots) should be the size of your palm and a serving of a lower-sugar vegetable (like broccoli or mushrooms)

should be the size of two palms. You could definitely go higher and be more exact; this is just a simple way to look at it.

Basically, what I just explained was how I ate to achieve my success. There is no one-size-fits-all way of eating, of course, and I'm not certain that low-carbohydrate eating would be sustainable for the long term for everyone, but I do believe that it could be beneficial to most people for a certain period of time. For example, if you were eating a lower-carbohydrate diet and it worked wonderfully, but then stopped working so well after a while, I think it's clear that you might need to make some changes, such as reintroducing more carbohydrates. It's all about being unafraid to keep experimenting until you find something that works for you.

ingredients

terms you should know

Although I define many terms in the coming pages, I am including some key definitions here to give you a foundation for understanding the information that follows, along with a few terms that I use often in the book that may be unfamiliar.

GMO

GMO is an acronym for genetically modified organism. GMOs are organisms whose genetic material has been altered to make them grow faster, be hardier, and even kill off bugs when they eat them. This manipulation can cause the organisms' genetic material to become unstable. The United States does not require companies to label whether an item is genetically modified or might contain GMO ingredients, even though GMOs are considered unsafe in many developed countries.

organic

A label established by the USDA guaranteeing that no hormones, antibiotics, synthetic pesticides, GMOs, or synthetic additives were used in the making of a product.

organically grown

This term typically applies to produce and other items that are commonly found at farmers' markets. It implies that the product was made in accordance with organic standards but does not have the official organic label. Organic certification costs a significant amount of money, and some farms are unable or unwilling to pay for it.

Umami might seem like a bizarre word, but I urge you to add it to your vocabulary. The word has Japanese roots and translates to "pleasant savory taste." Although its translation is rather plain, umami means much more than that. It's actually one of the five basic tastes; the other four are salty, sour, bitter, and sweet. It's directly related to the glutamate receptors in the body, which could be considered the body's sense of deliciousness—the kind that wakens your mind and makes you want to go back for another bite. It's somewhat like that ahh feeling when you step into a warm bath, but in the form of taste. Glutamate is found in different foods at different levels; this is why certain ingredients that are naturally higher in glutamate have more umami in them. These high-glutamate ingredients include fish sauce (one of my favorites), tomatoes, mushrooms, and cured meats like bacon. In the late 1800s, one of the world's most influential chefs, Auguste Escoffier, was one of the first people to utilize umami in cooking, although he didn't know the chemical source of it at the time. Later, in 1908, a Japanese scientist named Kikunae Ikeda identified it chemically and later gave it the name umami. This explanation may be long-winded, but that is how significant umami is to me!

foodie

A foodie is a person who has a tenacious love for food but is past the point of simply enjoying it. Foodies don't seek out food just for convenience or in response to hunger. Instead, they search for experiences and adventure through taste. Foodies typically have strong feelings toward certain foods and ingredients and can usually be relied on to join in on a restaurant run, though they are sometimes considered snobbish about food.

sourcing meat

Many scientific studies suggest that we humans evolved to eat meat, and I tend to agree. Despite arguments that people make against the decision, eating meat can be healthful, sustainable, and ethical. You simply have to know what to look for and where to look. Many high-ranking chefs and foodies claim that how an animal is raised and what it is fed are among the most important factors that determine how flavorful and nutritious the meat is. Before you buy meat, make it a priority to know how the animal was raised and what it ate.

pastured poultry, eggs, and pork

Poultry is a widely used term that defines all things bird. When it comes to poultry (including both meat and eggs) and pork, you want pastured.

Pastured tends to get mixed up with other terms like free-range and cage-free. As similar as they might sound, they couldn't be more contrasting. Pastured animals have the freedom to roam a pasture all day and live where they please. They're allowed to forage for food such as insects, grass, and other plants. (Many farms that raise pastured birds or pigs supplement with feed, which is acceptable because birds and pigs can eat and digest grains, unlike ruminants like cows and lambs. *Supplement* is the keyword here; the feed shouldn't make up the majority of their diet if you want truly pastured meat.) Sadly, terms like cage-free and free-range are just labeling gimmicks. Cage-free or free-range birds aren't caged, but instead are often crammed into large pens with no room to move. Of course they don't explain that part on the label.

You may have noticed that I didn't list organic pork or poultry. Organic certification is great for many reasons, but it is often used as a labeling gimmick. It's good because it ensures that no antibiotics or added hormones are used in the product and that the feed is organic, but it doesn't guarantee that the animals are raised properly, like being

on pasture. I suppose you could consider pastured poultry and pork as being beyond organic. I have such a great local source of pastured meats that I don't buy organic meats anymore, but not everyone has a source for pastured meats. If your only choice is organic, know that it is much better than conventionally raised pork or poultry, which is commonly full of synthetic hormones and antibiotics.

I prioritize pastured poultry and pork over organic, but if you do not have access or are unwilling to pay the premium, here's a list of how I choose to prioritize these meats:

1. Pastured

This is what I recommend to people who really care about the health benefits and flavor of their meat. You are most likely to find pastured meats through a local farmer, and it would be unusual to find any that is not antibiotic and hormone free. Because the animals live on a pasture, they have stronger immune systems and are less vulnerable to disease, so antibiotics are unlikely to be used. The excellent thing about purchasing from a local farm is that if you are concerned or curious, you can talk to the farmers and find out everything that goes on with the animals. They should be confident in answering your questions, whereas a corporation might not be.

2. Organic

Organic meat is far better than conventional, but why all the labels like vegetarian-fed, free-range, and so on? Pigs and poultry are omnivorous; therefore, they shouldn't be fed a vegetarian diet, if you ask me. The benefit of this choice is that a vegetarian diet ensures that no antibiotics or hormones were given to the animals and that they were fed an organic feed that is likely corn and soy based but is non-GMO and pesticide free. On rare occasion you might find organic pastured meat, but it's not easy to come by, and it's likely to be more expensive than pastured meat purchased from a local farm.

3. Natural/free-range/cage-free

In my opinion, these are labeling tricks that have people going head over heels for no reason. These terms make you think that the animals are at least given some time to move and suggest that they are not given antibiotics or hormones. Movies like *Food Inc.* have revealed that companies have used this label in misleading and fraudulent ways. If you choose meat labeled natural, free-range, or cage-free, try to get to know the company or farm you're buying it from so you know exactly what you're getting.

4. Conventional

There is no guarantee as to what comes with conventionally raised meat. It's likely that the animals are treated with hormones and/or antibiotics and are fed a GMO- and pesticide-laden feed. They are also likely to be kept in feedlots and crammed into uncomfortable spaces for most of their lives.

grass-fed beef and lamb

There is absolutely no comparison between grass-fed and grain-fed beef and lamb. Cows and lambs are biologically meant to eat grass. They can eat and live off grain, but it is so far off their natural diet that it messes up their fatty acid profile, resulting in much less healthful meat. But is that really that big of a deal? In my opinion it is. I believe that eating grass-fed meat can make you healthier for many reasons. Although fat isn't the problem, grass-fed beef and lamb are leaner than conventionally raised beef and lamb. Their fat is also much higher in healthy omega-3, the same fatty acid that is prevalent in salmon and other fatty fish. It is also higher in another healthy fat called conjugated linoleic acid, or CLA, which has been shown to reduce the risk of cancer and aid in the burning of fat. So if you're trying to lose weight or lean out, it may be wise to stick to grass-fed meat. Not to mention that it tastes far better than its conventionally raised counterpart!

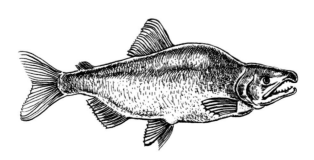

wild-caught seafood

Seafood is a little simpler. I strive to buy only sustainable wild-caught seafood because I prefer fish that was taken fresh from its natural habitat rather than raised in a tank. I never buy farm-raised seafood; I don't think it's a healthy decision. There is a big debate about whether it's more ethical to buy farm-raised fish, but I just don't feel comfortable with it because it's much lower in beneficial nutrients, it's typically fed GMO corn and soy and given antibiotics. In fact, farmed fish is fed more antibiotics per pound than any other conventionally raised animal in North America.

supporting local farms

I believe in supporting local farms whenever possible. You are much more likely to find grass-fed and pastured meats from local farms, and you'll probably enjoy and benefit more from the experience, too.

Two incredibly useful websites have helped me find farms located near me: eatwild.com and localharvest.com. Type in your zip code or city and state, and these sites will show you all the farms near you. You may stumble upon a multitude of great farms close by.

Lucky for me, my friend Leilani introduced me to a wonderful farm called Yonder Way that has become my go-to source for meat. The beautiful couple behind it, Jason and Lynsey, care so deeply about their animals, the way they are raised, and the quality of food for everyone that it melts my heart. After ordering from them for a while, I developed a great personal relationship with them. I'm truly honored to be able to call them my friends and am proud to purchase from them. Nothing feels better than to shake the hand of the person who handles the animals behind the food you eat with loving care and consideration. Not to mention that the transparency is incredibly liberating; you know exactly how the animals are treated and what they eat.

Since we began purchasing from Yonder Way, my family's appreciation for our food and where it comes from has swelled to the point that we make it a priority to know the origins of every ingredient we use in our kitchen. You have to experience this type of relationship between you, your food, and the people behind it to fully understand the closeness you achieve by buying from local farms. To me, good food cooked at home is one of the greatest expressions of love, because someone puts their work and emotions into the food in a way that reverberates through all of the body's senses: the smells drifting through the house, the sounds of clattering pots and pans, the appearance of food as it's delicately plated in front of you, the taste of the food as you savor every bite, the mouthfeel of comingling textures creating a wonderland of flavors that dance on the tongue as you enjoy the meal. The cooking of food and the growing or raising of food are not so different. Just as cooking is a form of expression, so is growing or raising food. When it's cared for diligently and thoughtfully, you can see and taste it; the food is better in every way. Some people may view meat with disgust or sadness, but to me, if it was properly raised, it is a thing of beauty and painstaking care. Jason and Lynsey have become a part of my family because of the role they play in my life, and I hope you can have the same kind of experience with a local farmer.

So why worry about all this? Is it just for health, or are there even more benefits? For me it's about two things: health and ethics. As an added benefit, meats from animals that are raised the way nature intended simply taste better, because their flavor is more pronounced and vibrant. I'm almost certain that if you try pastured or grass-fed meat or wild-caught fish, you won't feel compelled to go back. It takes experiencing the empowering act of supporting a local farmer, tasting the pronounced difference in the flavor of your food, and feeling great from eating properly and ethically raised foods to understand why the movement is so powerful.

buying produce

It's also important to consider where your produce comes from. Buy as many vegetables and fruits as possible organic or organically grown, which means that no synthetic pesticides, synthetic herbicides, or synthetic fertilizers were used in growing the produce. There is speculation that the pesticides and herbicides used in conventional farming may be linked to certain diseases and birth defects, making them potentially unsafe for consumption. Along with that, some conventionally grown produce is genetically modified, or GMO, which I also avoid whenever I can. I stick to organically grown produce from my farmers' market or organic produce from the grocery store.

That said, there are some gray areas when it comes to produce. For example, because avocados have thick skins, any pesticides or herbicides used never really penetrate to the flesh. That makes non-organic avocados technically safe. If you want to find out more about which produce is safe to buy conventionally so that you don't always have to go to the expense of buying organic, you can view a list of "clean" and "dirty" choices in terms of pesticide residue at ewg.org. Still, it's better to buy organic whenever you can.

the bottom line

So what does this all mean? How do you make decisions, and what should you consider? The way I see it, there are eight important things that you should ask yourself before making a decision about sourcing and eating food:

1. Do you know, respect, and appreciate where your food comes from?

2. Do you feel well informed about the food you eat?

3. After you have done your research, do you still feel compelled to buy the same ingredients, and will you continue to eat the same way?

4. Are you completely comfortable with how the animals you eat are treated and what they are fed?

5. Are you eating the meat and produce that you buy with confidence rather than blindness?

6. For your own health and the health of your family, do you believe that it's practical to make a change if necessary?

7. Is supporting your local economy by buying locally important to you?

8. Have you at least tried purchasing and consuming sustainable, local food to come to a decision on whether any extra expense or effort is worth it to you?

my final say

Eat real food. Eat animals that were raised in a biologically appropriate way in a happy and healthy environment. Eat plenty of fresh organically raised plants along with animals. Avoid products that contain unnecessary additives such as preservatives and ridiculous amounts of sugar. If you cannot pronounce or identify something on a product's ingredient list, it's probably a good idea to skip it. Stick to foods that are good for you, and find ways to enjoy them. And don't forget to indulge every once in a while.

If you're interested in learning more about food, I highly recommend the documentary *Food Inc.* It's incredibly informative and covers many issues surrounding the food industry in the United States. There are also great sources of information online, like chriskresser.com and marksdailyapple.com. Chris Kresser provides excellent information about heated food-related debates with substantial amounts of scientific evidence. Mark Sisson, who runs Mark's Daily Apple, has a vast database filled with answers to just about any question you might have when it comes to healthy eating and living.

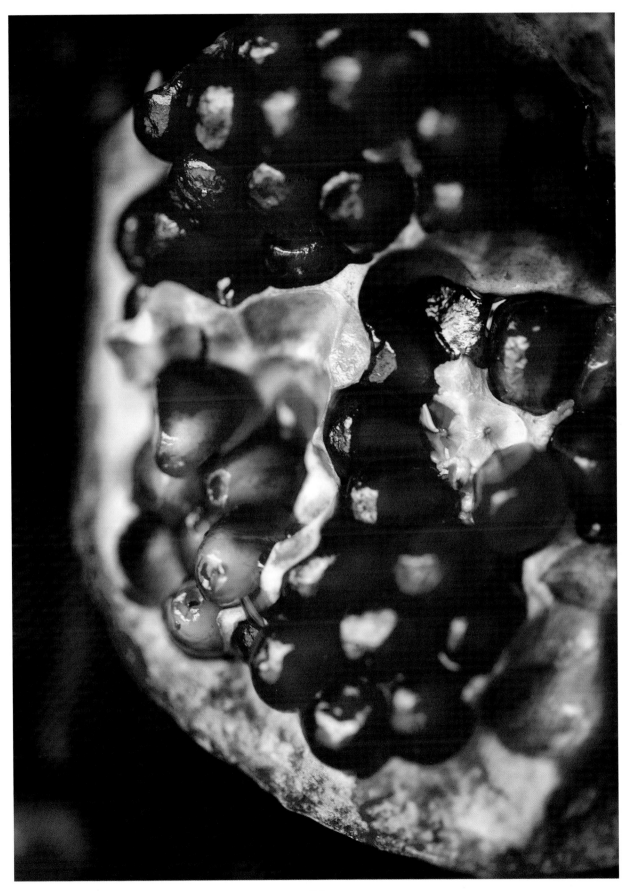

shopping for pantry ingredients

cooking fats

I use a plethora of flavorful and versatile fats in the kitchen, from avocado oil to lard. The key is to use cooking fats selectively, not just for flavor but also to suit the cooking method and temperature. I prefer to use saturated fats—typically animal fats or ghee—for high-temperature cooking like searing and roasting because they are more heat stable at high temperatures. While avocado oil is an unsaturated fat, it tends to be more resistant to heat than others, which is why I use it occasionally for things like roasting vegetables, but only if I'm short on other cooking fats. I used to cook with extra-virgin olive oil, but now I utilize it only for cold uses, like on a salad, for finishing a plated dish, and occasionally to simmer in a sauce. I made this choice after learning that olive oil is susceptible to oxidative damage and loses beneficial nutrients at high temperatures, not to mention that it also has a smoke point of around 350 degrees, which isn't very high. That doesn't scare me from putting it in a simmering tomato sauce, but I prefer not to use it to sear foods in a hot pan or roast foods at a high temperature. For cooking I use the following fats (see the sources section on page 263 for more information):

pastured lard

Lard is the rendered fat of a pig. You can buy pork fat from your local farmer or butcher and render it yourself, or buy it pre-rendered from a good source like Fatworks. While we aren't afraid of saturated fat anymore, it is interesting to note that lard is around half monounsaturated fat, which is the same type of fat found in avocados, olive oil, and nuts. Lard does have a subtle "porky" taste, but it gives a wonderful flavor to many dishes, especially roasted vegetables.

grass-fed tallow

Tallow is similar to lard but comes from rendering cow fat rather than pig fat. You can obtain it the same way you obtain lard. Grass-fed tallow is incredibly rich in omega-3 fatty acids, which promote heart function and provide CLA, which has been proven to reduce body fat and increase lean muscle mass. Similar to pork fat, tallow has a mild "beefy" flavor that tastes quite nice when used selectively in certain dishes. I prefer to brown my steaks in tallow to keep the flavor tone neutral.

grass-fed ghee

Ghee is one of my favorite and most often used cooking fats because it is fairly mild tasting and is very versatile for both browning and sautéing. Ghee is a type of clarified butter, which is made by removing the milk solids and water from unsalted butter, leaving nothing but the golden butterfat. With the milk solids removed, ghee is much more heat stable and has a much higher smoke point than butter. You can make it yourself or order it from a trusted source like Pure Indian Foods. If you want to make it yourself, I have a tutorial on my website (slimpalate.com).

grass-fed butter

I think we all know what butter is, but I would like to take a moment to explain where I source my butter. Finding local grass-fed butter can be difficult, but there are a couple of brands that I trust and use when I can't get it locally: Kerrygold and Smjör.

avocado oil

Look for cold-pressed avocado oil without additives. I don't usually cook with avocado oil except for the occasional roasting of vegetables in the oven at no higher than 400 degrees. I use it for sautéing or browning only when I have no other cooking fats on hand, which is rare. I prefer to use avocado oil when I need a fat that will remain liquid when mixed with another liquid, such as in a marinade. Avocado oil has a mild "green" scent and a light avocado flavor tone. That avocado flavor tone tends to mellow a bit and usually isn't noticeable when the avocado oil is cooked into things, so don't worry about using it in marinades or for roasting in the oven, as the flavor shouldn't overpower the dish. Avocado oil can also be used in a vinaigrette or salad dressing to give it a subtle and fresh avocado finish.

organic coconut oil

Look for cold-pressed extra-virgin coconut oil. It can be used in place of butter in many recipes if you are lactose intolerant. Even though I'm not lactose intolerant, I choose to use coconut oil on occasion in dishes like sautéed vegetables just to change things up. Some people find that coconut oil has a slightly sweet and coconutty taste; it can be slightly noticeable to me. Then again, coconut oil has only very light coconut notes that are usually too mellow to overpower the other flavors in a dish, assuming that they're strong, like garlic. I've also noticed that it sometimes depends on the container of coconut oil you happen to get; some containers seem to have a little more coconut pulp in them than others. Even though the coconut pulp is minimal, it does contribute to the strength of the coconut flavor.

dairy

Wait a minute—dairy isn't Paleo! Okay, here is my stance on this: I believe that Paleo is a template for finding what makes you feel good and fit. I tolerate dairy just fine, so instead of eliminating a perfectly healthy and delicious ingredient, I choose to use it. I stick to grass-fed sources for all dairy, especially butter, because it is reflected so much in the flavor of the finished dish. Typically I buy my dairy from local farms, but some products are difficult to get locally, like yogurt and butter. Luckily there are a few trustworthy grass-fed brands out there, which you can find listed in the sources section on page 263.

If you buy your dairy from a local farm, it is likely raw, which means that it has not been pasteurized and still contains some of the beneficial nutrients and healthy cultures that are good for your digestive system. These nutrients and cultures can easily be killed off in the pasteurization process. Another great benefit of consuming raw dairy is that some people who cannot tolerate pasteurized dairy can tolerate raw dairy. If you have an intolerance to dairy, you may want to give raw dairy a try. Goat milk dairy is another option.

When it comes to dairy, this book's recipes use mainly butter, but a few use heavy cream, yogurt, or cheese. If you want to avoid dairy and/or have a serious intolerance to it, I have made it optional or include a substitution for it in the recipes that use it. If no substitution is given for something like butter or heavy cream, I would say it's safe to assume you that can substitute another cooking fat for the butter and coconut milk for the heavy cream, but I wouldn't exactly advise it unless you absolutely must. Substitutions for any dairy used in a recipe typically change the flavor profile and texture of the dish substantially.

milks

--------- almond milk ---------

Almond milk is made by soaking almonds in water overnight, grinding it all up with some more water, and then filtering out the almond pulp from the liquid, leaving you with almond milk. In all of my recipes, I use unsweetened almond milk. I typically make my own almond milk to avoid preservatives and inflammatory additives; you can find my recipe on my blog, slimpalate.com. If you buy almond milk, make sure to purchase the unsweetened variety.

--------- coconut milk ---------

Coconut milk is made similarly to almond milk with its filtering process. It is a much better substitute for heavy cream (although still not recommended in terms of recipe results unless you can't tolerate dairy), as it's much thicker and fattier than almond milk. Whenever I use coconut milk, I use the full-fat variety, which has the best texture and flavor. Look for brands that are free of BPA, like Native Forest, Natural Value, and the Aroy-D tetra paks. Native Forest does contain a little bit of guar gum, but most people can tolerate it without experiencing any digestive issues. If you happen to be one of the few who can't, then you can turn to one of the other two brands.

sweeteners

--------- pure honey ---------

When using sweeteners, I like to stick to the most raw and basic forms, such as honey. I occasionally use coconut sugar, maple sugar, or organic cane sugar, but I stick mainly to honey when it comes to sweets (which I indulge in very rarely). I like to purchase honey at my local farmers' market because it's always raw and fresh. If you buy it from the store, look out for sugar additives, and make sure to choose pure honey. Honey is sweeter than sugar, so when substituting honey in a recipe that calls for sugar, I usually use a ratio of 1:2, meaning ½ cup honey in place of 1 cup sugar.

pure liquid stevia

Stevia is an herb that is commonly grown for its sweet leaves. It is about 300 times sweeter than sugar and has a negligible effect on blood sugar. You definitely want to avoid any majorly processed or artificial sweetener that is not pure stevia extract. Watch out for stevia brands that have added ingredients like dextrose; look for brands that are pure stevia extract. My favorite is SweetLeaf Liquid Stevia Sweet Drops.

During my weight loss journey, I didn't even eat honey because it is so high in sugar, even though it's a natural sugar. It was easier to eliminate it altogether than to take on the task of moderating it so heavily. As I've mentioned before, just because it's real food and has health benefits does not mean that it will help you lose weight, if that is your goal. If you're trying to lose weight, it's better to get your occasional sweet fix with stevia.

coconut palm sugar

Although it's used in only one recipe in this book, I wanted to touch base on coconut palm sugar, also known as coconut sugar. It is made from the crystallized nectar of coconut palm tree flowers and has a somewhat caramel-like flavor that I would compare to brown sugar. An interesting fact about this sugar is that it's a lower-glycemic sweetener than cane sugar, maple syrup, honey, and so on. It also contains nutrients such as amino acids, magnesium, potassium, iron, zinc, and B vitamins. Don't let my explanation fool you, though; coconut palm sugar is still a sweetener and still contains sugar. My favorite brand is Navitas Naturals, which seems to be widely available in supermarkets.

flours and thickeners

almond flour

In all my recipes that call for almond flour, I use Honeyville blanched almond flour. It's one of the finest-ground almond flours you can buy, which yields the best results in baking. I don't recommend using almond meal in any of this book's recipes; using almond meal results in a completely different texture, and dishes don't always bake correctly or evenly. That said, it is not a sin to use almond meal in place of almond flour if you are prepared for altered results.

coconut flour

I like to use coconut flour because it gives baked goods a gorgeous cakey texture with minimal coconutty flavor. You have to be careful with coconut flour, though; you can't really substitute it for anything else. Coconut flour absorbs a massive amount of liquid, which means that the recipe must contain quite a bit of liquid and eggs for good results. For nice cakey results, I typically use a ratio of about 4 eggs and ½ cup liquid, whether it's almond milk mixed with liquid stevia or honey, to ½ cup coconut flour.

arrowroot starch

Typically I use arrowroot starch as a replacement for cornstarch in minimal amounts and for thickening sauces. I usually stick to about 1 teaspoon to 1 tablespoon of the fine white powder, depending on how thick I want the sauce. Just be sure to wait until the sauce cools a little bit before adding it, as its thickening properties don't seem to activate as well if the sauce is boiling. If you want to thicken a larger quantity of sauce by a lot, I recommend mixing the arrowroot starch with a little bit of water and some of the hot liquid before adding it to the sauce, which makes the thickening properties act faster and makes it more soluble.

flavorings

coconut aminos or tamari

Tamari is a soy sauce made from fermented soybeans rather than wheat. I tend to avoid soy, so I typically use coconut aminos as a substitute for both tamari and soy sauce. But I do use a little tamari on occasion because it's fermented; soy that is unfermented has poisonous and potentially hormone-destroying properties. In terms of flavor, you can use an equal amount of tamari in place of soy sauce, but the same cannot be said about coconut aminos. Coconut aminos tends to give a dish a slightly sweet flavor, so I don't recommend substituting an equal amount of coconut aminos for tamari or soy sauce. Instead, I usually mix a little bit of salty fish sauce into my coconut aminos to balance out the sweetness, typically a 2:1 ratio of coconut aminos to fish sauce.

fish sauce

Fish sauce is a liquid that's extracted by fermenting fish with sea salt in a giant wooden vat. While it may sound strange, it's an incredibly versatile ingredient that adds a massive amount of umami and depth of flavor to any dish. It can be utilized in sauces, marinades, soups, vinaigrettes, on vegetables . . . really, the uses of fish sauce are limited only by the mind. The only brand I use is Red Boat Fish Sauce. Many other fish sauce brands contain sugar, which in my opinion throws off the flavor and therefore should be avoided. Red Boat Fish Sauce is made from only wild-caught anchovies and sea salt.

salt

Regular sea salt and Himalayan salt are both great salts to use in cooking, and neither imparts any flavor of its own. I prefer unflavored sea salts, but I enjoy smoked sea salt on occasion when I want a dish to have a smoky flavor profile. When cooking I prefer coarsely ground sea salt rather than very finely ground because it's easier to gauge how much you are salting your dishes. If you use fine-ground sea salt when salting something that's just slightly damp on the outside, like meat or vegetables, or something that is in the middle of cooking, the salt dissolves on contact and you can't see it anymore. This makes it difficult to tell how much you've salted it, which often results in either oversalting or undersalting whatever it is you're making. Watch out for brands that contain additives like flowing agents and dextrose; your sea salt should consist of only one thing: sea salt.

unsweetened cacao powder

Cacao powder is essentially the same thing as cocoa powder. Cacao powder is simply the least processed and most raw form of cocoa powder, meaning that it has more of its nutrients intact. You can substitute regular unsweetened cocoa powder if you wish, but I prefer and recommend unsweetened cacao powder, and that's what I've used in these recipes.

extra-virgin olive oil

I've put extra-virgin olive oil in flavorings rather than cooking fats because, as mentioned previously, I typically do not cook with it. I like to keep its full flavor intact by reserving it mainly for cold uses, with the exception of very-low-heat cooking such as simmering in a tomato sauce. It works wonderfully not only in vinaigrettes but also as a finishing touch to many dishes. Using a small drizzle of olive oil over soups, fish, and meats just before serving livens up the flavor of the dish with subtle spicy and bitter notes and gives it a mild, earthy, and olive-y finish. There are many brands to choose from at the supermarket, but a large majority of them are not truly extra-virgin. You want cold-pressed 100% extra-virgin olive oil, though even then it's possible that it's not actually extra-virgin. Because finding true extra-virgin olive oil is difficult, I recommend finding a good local source. If you can't find one, then one of the few distributed olive oils that I trust and use is Kasandrinos Extra Virgin Olive Oil.

breakfast

breakfast sausage and broccoli nested eggs

Eggs are one of my favorite foods because of their versatility. In my family, nothing is really limited to just breakfast. I enjoy eggs whenever I feel the necessity to, which is quite often, and usually in a nest of vegetables. Nesting the eggs sunny side up in vegetables gives you a one-pan breakfast that you can just put on a plate and enjoy. These eggs are embedded in crispy homemade breakfast sausage and tender broccoli, making for a fast and easy morning meal, or even a lunch or dinner.

for the breakfast sausage:

- 1 pound pork
- 2 cloves garlic, minced
- ¼ teaspoon nutmeg
- 1 teaspoon chopped fresh thyme
- ¼ teaspoon chopped fresh rosemary
- 1 tablespoon chopped fresh sage
- ½ teaspoon mustard powder
- ¼ teaspoon cinnamon
- 1 teaspoon salt
- ½ teaspoon pepper
- ¼ teaspoon red pepper flakes

- 2 teaspoons ghee or coconut oil
- 2 cups broccoli florets, cut into uniform pieces
- 5 eggs
- salt and pepper to taste

1. In a medium-sized bowl, mix all the breakfast sausage ingredients until well combined. Refrigerate, covered with foil or plastic wrap, for at least 4 hours, but preferably overnight.

2. In a large skillet, heat the ghee or coconut oil over medium heat. Add the broccoli and cook, stirring occasionally, for 5—6 minutes or until the broccoli starts to become tender. Add the sausage, increase the heat to medium-high, and cook for 5 minutes, stirring occasionally, until the sausage is browned and cooked through.

3. Make 5 pockets in the sausage and broccoli mixture by pushing it apart. Crack an egg into each pocket, season with salt and pepper, then cover the pan with a tight-fitting lid or foil and cook for 3—4 minutes or until the whites are set.

Note: I like to make the breakfast sausage the night before I make this dish so that it's ready to use for breakfast when I wake up in the morning. You can also freeze the sausage for use another time.

pancakes with almond butter
and blackberry sauce

I have never known anyone who doesn't like some form of pancakes. Some people like them drenched in processed and sugar-laden syrups, and others like them with just a handful of berries on top. When we were kids my brother always covered his pancakes with peanut butter and strawberry syrup. I had to do the same thing, of course, and it was amazing! With this childhood favorite in mind, I made a version with creamy almond butter and a fresh blackberry sauce so that I could once again enjoy the culinary creation that captured my heart so long ago—but without the sugary syrup. This is essentially the "peanut butter and jelly" version of pancakes, but we can pretend that it's very sophisticated.

for the blackberry sauce:

- 6 ounces blackberries
- 7 drops liquid stevia or 1 tablespoon honey

for the pancakes:

- ¼ cup coconut flour, sifted
- 1 teaspoon baking soda
- pinch of salt
- 4 eggs
- ¾ teaspoon pure vanilla extract
- ¼ cup unsweetened almond milk or coconut milk
- 1 tablespoon honey
- ghee for frying
- ⅓ cup almond butter

1. In a blender, purée the blackberries until completely smooth. Pour through a mesh sieve, pushing against the sieve until most of the liquid has strained through, then discard the seeds. Stir the stevia or honey into the blackberry purée.

2. In a medium-sized bowl, combine the coconut flour, baking soda, and salt and stir with a fork to incorporate. In a separate bowl, whisk together the eggs, vanilla, almond or coconut milk, and honey. Pour the wet mixture into the dry mixture and stir until thoroughly incorporated and no lumps remain.

3. Heat about a tablespoon of ghee in a large pan over medium heat, then ladle in the batter to make 2—3 inch pancakes, making sure to space them far enough apart that they don't connect. Cook the pancakes for 2—3 minutes or until they begin to bubble, then flip them and cook for another 2 minutes. Place the pancakes on a warmed tray lined with paper towels, and repeat the process with the remaining batter.

4. Serve the pancakes with almond butter and blackberry sauce spooned on top.

spinach and grape tomato frittata with basil and goat cheese

On weekends when everything is mellow and the scent of fresh-brewed coffee drifts into my room, I almost always make breakfast for my parents after waking up. One of our favorite meals on these coffee-scented mornings is a frittata. It's hard to beat a delicate and fluffy mass of farm-fresh eggs studded with vegetables and herbs from the farmers' market. Using simple yet distinctive ingredients, this light frittata lets each ingredient shine.

- 7 eggs
- 1½ tablespoons heavy cream or coconut milk
- salt and pepper to taste
- 11 large basil leaves
- 1 cup halved grape tomatoes
- 3 tablespoons crumbled goat cheese (optional)
- 1½ cups packed baby spinach
- 2 tablespoons butter or ghee

1. Preheat the oven to 425°F.

2. In a medium-sized bowl, add the eggs, heavy cream or coconut milk, and salt and pepper and whisk until thoroughly combined. Stack 8 of the basil leaves, roll the stack tightly like a cigar, slice into thin ribbons, and place in a small bowl along with the halved grape tomatoes, goat cheese (if using), and spinach.

3. Heat the butter or ghee in a medium-sized oven-safe pan over medium-low heat. Add the egg mixture to the pan. Slowly and continuously stir with a heat-proof silicone spatula for about 3 minutes or until the egg begins to set, but don't scramble. Slowly stir in the grape tomato and spinach mixture until well dispersed and let cook, untouched, for 3—4 minutes or until the edges are set.

4. Transfer the pan to the oven and bake for 5—7 minutes or until the center is set. Remove from the oven and let cool for 5 minutes. Serve hot or at room temperature.

Note: I have made the goat cheese optional for those who do not eat any dairy, but I must admit that this dish truly is not the same without it.

coconut breakfast muffin

serves 1

When I'm in need of a muffin fix and don't have time to bake some in the oven, I turn to this recipe. I don't like to utilize the microwave too often, but it is a surprisingly versatile tool in this situation. This recipe is as simple as a few ingredients mixed in a ramekin and placed in the microwave, and it comes out an airy, light, and slightly sweet muffin that is perfect for a nice spread of creamy almond butter or smashed berries.

- 1 teaspoon coconut oil
- 1 egg
- 1 tablespoon coconut flour, sifted
- 1 tablespoon unsweetened almond milk
- 5 drops liquid stevia or ½ teaspoon honey
- 1 tablespoon pumpkin puree (optional)

1. Grease a medium-sized ramekin with the coconut oil.

2. In a small bowl, combine the egg, coconut flour, almond milk, stevia or honey, and pumpkin, if using, stirring until fully incorporated. Pour the batter into the greased ramekin and microwave on high for 2 minutes.

3. Carefully pop the muffin out of the ramekin. Serve with your spread of choice, or just eat it by itself.

prosciutto egg cups

Bacon is one of the most powerful flavors you can add to your food, but I've noticed that its friend prosciutto and other cured meats are sadly neglected. Prosciutto is essentially the same as bacon, but it is made from the leg of the pig rather than the belly, dried instead of smoked, and usually cured only in salt, without a sweetener such as maple syrup or brown sugar. In this recipe, I line muffin cups with prosciutto and bake eggs inside the prosciutto-lined cups, which results in a soft-cooked egg with a salty, crunchy, and meaty shell around it.

- avocado oil or melted ghee for greasing the muffin pan
- 8 slices prosciutto
- 3½ tablespoons chopped fresh chives
- 3½ ounces grated cheddar cheese (optional)
- 8 eggs
- salt and pepper to taste

1. Preheat the oven to 375°F and lightly grease 8 cups of a muffin pan with the avocado oil or melted ghee.

2. Line each muffin cup with 1 slice of prosciutto, covering the bottom and sides completely. Divide the chives and cheddar cheese, if using, among the prosciutto-lined muffin cups, then crack 1 egg into each cup.

3. Season each egg with salt and pepper and bake for 15 minutes until the egg whites are opaque. Loosen from the muffin cups carefully with a butter knife and serve immediately, or store in the fridge for up to 4 days.

oeufs en cocette

This is a fun recipe to make on weekends or weekdays because it's fast and easy yet presents very elegantly. Perfectly baked eggs are nestled in a ramekin with an herbed surprise beneath them. I like to serve these with freshly cooked vegetables for dipping into the broken and oozing yolks.

- melted ghee or softened butter for greasing the ramekin
- 2 green onions, thinly sliced, divided
- 2 teaspoons minced fresh rosemary, divided
- 3 tablespoons crumbled goat cheese, divided (optional)
- 4 eggs, divided
- 4 tablespoons heavy cream or coconut milk, divided
- salt and pepper to taste

1. Preheat the oven to 375°F and grease two 8-ounce ramekins with melted ghee or softened butter.

2. In the bottom of one ramekin, add half of the green onion, rosemary, and goat cheese, if using. Crack an egg into the ramekin and add 1 tablespoon of the heavy cream or coconut milk, then crack the other egg and add the remaining 1 tablespoon heavy cream or coconut milk. Repeat with the second ramekin.

3. Season with salt and pepper, and bake for 15–20 minutes or until the egg whites are opaque.

Note: This recipe can easily be doubled, tripled, or quadrupled to feed multiple people. Since it's done in individual ramekins, there is no need to change the cooking time.

soft scrambled eggs with mushrooms and chives

If I'm going to have scrambled eggs, I want them soft scrambled. I don't much enjoy scrambled eggs that have dry, lifeless, and gigantic curds stacked on top of one another. Constantly stirring the eggs in the pan during cooking breaks them down, creating very small curds and resulting in the silkiest, creamiest eggs you'll ever have.

- 2½ tablespoons butter or ghee, divided
- 8 ounces mushrooms, sliced
- 8 eggs
- salt and pepper to taste
- 1 tablespoon heavy cream or coconut milk
- ¼ cup chopped fresh chives

1. In a small pan over medium heat, heat 1 tablespoon of the butter or ghee. Sauté the mushrooms for 4—5 minutes or until completely cooked.

2. In a separate medium-sized pan, melt 1 tablespoon of the butter or ghee over medium heat. Crack the eggs into the pan, whisking until the yolks are completely mixed into the whites. Cook for 2 minutes, continuously stirring briskly with a heat-proof scraper, until the eggs begin to thicken. Take the pan off the heat, continuing to stir and scrape, then add the remaining ½ tablespoon butter or ghee and season with salt and pepper. Place the pan back on the heat for 1—2 more minutes, still stirring and scraping, until small curds start to form and a creamy texture develops.

3. Whisk in the heavy cream or coconut milk and immediately take the pan off the heat. Stir in the chives and cooked mushrooms and serve immediately.

 Note: If the eggs begin to set to quickly, take them off the heat earlier while stirring, returning them to the heat and off the heat again until they are thick and creamy.

bacon and caramelized shallot quiche

My mother loves quiche and becomes weak in the knees whenever she sees some within her grasp. Combining salty bacon and sweet caramelized shallots creates a salty-sweet contrast that gives the filling of this quiche a wonderful umami flavor. To go with the filling, I made a simple crust consisting of a little bit of almond flour, zucchini, and egg, because I doubt my mom would eat anything labeled as a quiche that didn't have a crust. Luckily, she approved of this creation and happily claimed a second slice as her own.

for the crust:

- butter or softened ghee for greasing the pie pan
- 2 medium zucchini, shredded
- ¼ cup blanched almond flour
- 2 eggs

for the filling:

- 2 tablespoons butter or ghee
- 4 shallots, thinly sliced
- 5 eggs
- ½ cup heavy cream or coconut milk
- 6 strips bacon, cooked and chopped
- ½ cup chopped arugula
- ½ cup grated cheddar cheese (optional)
- salt and pepper to taste

1. Preheat the oven to 350°F. Grease a 9-inch pie pan with the butter or softened ghee.

2. In a medium-sized bowl, mix all the ingredients for the crust. Press into the greased pie pan and bake for 20—25 minutes or until set and slightly browned.

3. Pull the crust out of the oven and increase the oven temperature to 375°F. Heat the butter or ghee in a medium-sized pan over medium-low heat and cook the shallots for 10 minutes or until nicely caramelized.

4. In a large bowl, whisk together the eggs, heavy cream or coconut milk, bacon, arugula, caramelized shallots, cheddar cheese (if using), and salt and pepper. Pour the egg mixture into the baked crust and bake for 25 minutes or until set.

rosemary fried eggs with garlic-lemon spinach

There are many ways to cook an egg, but frying is by far my favorite method. I typically fry my eggs in bacon fat reserved from cooking bacon previously; throwing out rendered bacon fat is a sin! When eggs are properly fried over easy, they should have golden brown and crispy edges and undersides but soft and ready-to-burst yolks. Infusing them with rosemary and placing them on a bed of wilted spinach takes these eggs to a slightly higher level. The second you cut into them, the yolks ooze all over the spinach, creating a wondrous velvety sauce.

for the spinach:

- ½ tablespoon butter or ghee
- 3 cloves garlic, thinly sliced
- 5 ounces spinach (about 2½ cups)
- juice of ½ lemon

for the eggs:

- 2½ tablespoons butter or ghee
- 4 eggs
- salt and pepper to taste
- 3 sprigs rosemary

1. In a medium-sized pan over medium heat, heat ½ tablespoon butter or ghee, then add the garlic and cook until fragrant. Add the spinach and cook, stirring often, until completely wilted. Squeeze the lemon juice over the wilted spinach and turn off the heat.

2. Heat 2½ tablespoons butter or ghee in a large frying pan until very hot. It's best to fry the eggs in batches to avoid overcrowding the pan. Bruise the rosemary sprigs and place them in the cooking fat near the eggs, but not directly on top of the uncooked whites or yolks. Fry each egg for 2—3 minutes, flicking hot cooking fat onto the whites with a spoon until they are completely opaque. Season with salt and pepper. Serve the eggs on top of the spinach.

mini cinnamon scones

Scones used to be a staple in my house, although they were from Starbucks and there wasn't anything special about them. When I changed my eating habits, I missed having those chewy, crumbly pastries with a coffee on the side, but didn't miss my former self. Instead of pouting about it, I made my own version with almond flour. These cinnamon scones have a smooth, golden exterior with a light and chewy inside, and they are coated with salty-sweet cinnamon butter. They are great as a breakfast treat with coffee and eggs.

for the scones:

- 2 cups blanched almond flour
- 1 teaspoon baking soda
- 1 teaspoon cinnamon
- pinch of salt
- 1 egg
- ½ teaspoon pure vanilla extract
- 2 tablespoons honey or 15 drops liquid stevia mixed with 2 tablespoons unsweetened almond milk

for the cinnamon butter:

- 2 tablespoons butter or ghee
- 1 teaspoon cinnamon
- 2 teaspoons honey or 10 drops liquid stevia
- pinch of salt

1. Preheat the oven to 350°F and line a baking sheet with parchment paper.

2. In a medium-sized bowl, combine the almond flour, baking soda, cinnamon, and salt. In a separate bowl, whisk together the egg, vanilla, and honey or stevia with almond milk. Pour the wet ingredients into the dry ingredients and mix until thoroughly combined. Form the dough into a 5-inch-long rectangle on the parchment-lined baking sheet.

3. With a knife long enough to cut all the way through widthwise, slice the dough into 3 even sections, being careful not to pull the sections apart. Then cut the entire rectangle in half lengthwise, giving you 6 even squares. Slice each square diagonally to get 12 mini scones.

4. Bake for 10–15 minutes or until golden around the edges. Let cool on a wire rack for at least 5 minutes.

5. In a small saucepan over medium heat, melt the butter or ghee. Mix in the cinnamon, honey or stevia, and salt. Serve the scones with the cinnamon butter spooned on top.

curried mini frittatas
with asparagus

I love frittatas. I enjoy serving a standard-sized frittata for brunch, but sometimes I like to switch things up and make miniature individual frittatas to serve. By using a muffin pan rather than a pie pan you get individual servings of fluffy egg that are fun and easy to serve at a party or take on the road. Each little frittata is studded with pieces of tender asparagus, and the addition of curry powder gives it an alluring fragrance.

- 1 tablespoon ghee, plus more for greasing the muffin pan
- 1 pound asparagus, trimmed
- 8 eggs
- 2 teaspoons curry powder
- 2 bunches green onions, sliced thinly
- 1 teaspoon tomato paste
- ¼ cup heavy cream or coconut milk
- salt and pepper to taste

1. In a medium-sized pan, melt the ghee. Add the asparagus and sauté for 6—7 minutes or until tender. Let cool for 5 minutes, then chop the asparagus into 1-inch pieces.

2. In a medium-sized bowl, mix all the ingredients until thoroughly combined. Grease a 12-cup mini muffin pan with ghee, pour the egg mixture into the greased muffin cups, and bake for 17—20 minutes or until the eggs are completely set. Serve immediately or store in the fridge for up to 1 week.

leek omelet with smoked salmon

There is no wrong way to make an omelet, but there are some specifications that I prefer. I make two types when introducing people to properly cooked omelets: a French *omelette,* which has no browning, has very small curds, and is very soft on the inside; and a country omelet, which is browned, has larger curds, and is slightly moist on the inside. I prefer a country omelet that is a little moist on the inside with a slightly crispy and nutty browned outside. This omelet meets those standards with a buttery and fragrant cooked fold of egg perked up with a velvety filling of salty smoked salmon and tart goat cheese.

- 1 medium leek
- 2½ teaspoons butter, divided
- 2 or 3 eggs
- 1 teaspoon heavy cream or coconut milk
- 1½ tablespoons minced fresh thyme
- salt and pepper to taste
- 1 ounce smoked salmon, sliced
- 2 tablespoons crumbled goat cheese (optional)

1. Cut off and discard the bottom root part and the green hard part of the leek (or save them for making stock). Slice the remaining part of the leek in half lengthwise and then into slices about ⅓-inch thick. Place the sliced leeks in a medium-sized bowl, fill with water, and swish the water around to rinse off any dirt. Drain the water and pat the leeks dry with a paper towel.

2. Melt 1½ teaspoons of the butter in a pan over medium heat, then sauté the leeks for 4−5 minutes or until they begin to soften. Crack the eggs in a medium-sized bowl, add the heavy cream or coconut milk, thyme, and salt and pepper, and whisk thoroughly until slightly frothy. Pour the egg mixture into the pan with the leeks and swish around to evenly distribute the egg mixture.

3. As the egg mixture cooks, gently pull the cooked egg to the center, refilling the empty pocket of the pan by allowing the egg mixture to fill it or by tilting the pan in the direction of the pocket. Continue until the egg mixture is mostly solid, with only a little liquid left.

4. Add the sliced salmon and crumbled goat cheese, if using, for the filling, and carefully fold the omelet in half. Add the remaining 1 teaspoon butter to the closed side of the omelet and tilt the pan to allow the butter to run under the omelet. Let it brown for 30 seconds.

5. Turn off the heat and pull out a plate for serving. Grip the handle underhanded and tap it against a hard surface so that the omelet comes to the edge of the pan. Hold the plate up to the pan and carefully invert the omelet onto the plate.

—— poultry ——

braised moroccan chicken
with stuffed green olives

serves 4—6

When I first discovered the beauty of braising, I began braising everything in sight. I couldn't get enough of this technique; in fact, I still can't. My parents rave about their experiences in Morocco, so I researched Morocco's cuisine and noticed Moroccan chicken showing up a lot. Many of the recipes used dates or raisins and were on the sweeter side, but I wanted something a little more fresh and zesty, so I made mine with a Moroccan spice mix along with classic aromatics flecked with vibrant pepper-stuffed green olives. This wonderful and easy braise is perfect for a get-together or a weeknight meal.

for the spice mix:

- ¼ teaspoon red pepper flakes
- ¼ teaspoon smoked paprika
- ½ teaspoon ground cumin
- ½ teaspoon ground ginger
- ¼ teaspoon ground coriander
- ¼ teaspoon pepper
- 8 saffron threads, crushed
- ¼ teaspoon salt

- 1 (3½–4 pound) chicken, cut into 8 pieces (breasts, thighs, legs, and wings)
- salt and pepper to taste
- 3 tablespoons ghee, divided
- 1 medium onion, sliced thinly
- 3 cloves garlic, sliced thinly
- ¾ cup water
- 3 tablespoons chopped fresh cilantro, divided
- 1 tablespoon chopped fresh parsley, divided
- 1 lemon, halved
- ½ cup green olives stuffed with red peppers, with 2 tablespoons olive juice
- ½ teaspoon arrowroot starch (optional)

1. In a small bowl, mix together all the spice mix ingredients. Rinse and pat dry the chicken, then season lightly with salt and pepper.

2. Heat 2 tablespoons of the ghee in a large Dutch oven or deep skillet with a lid over medium-high heat. Brown the chicken in batches so as not to overcrowd the Dutch oven, about 3—4 minutes per side or until it has a nice golden brown color. Place the chicken on a medium-sized dish and tent with foil.

3. Once all the chicken pieces are browned, reduce the heat to medium. Add the remaining 1 tablespoon ghee to the Dutch oven and stir in the onion and garlic. Cook for 2—3 minutes or until the onion and garlic begin to soften, then add the spice mix and cook for another minute or so, stirring frequently to prevent burning. Add the water, scraping the bottom of the Dutch oven with a wooden spoon. Bring to a light simmer, then add the chicken thighs, legs, and wings, but reserve the breasts. Reduce the heat to low, cover, and braise for 10 minutes. Then nestle in the chicken breasts (place them on top of the other pieces if there is no room), sprinkle half of the cilantro and parsley and squeeze the juice of one of the lemon halves over the top, cover, and braise for 20 minutes. Add the olives and olive juice, cover once more, and braise for 10—15 minutes or until the juices run clear when the chicken is pierced with a fork.

4. Remove the chicken to a warmed dish and tent with foil to keep warm. Turn the heat on the Dutch oven to medium-high and let the liquid reduce by about a third, then squeeze in the juice from the remaining lemon half and stir in the remaining cilantro and parsley. If you want it thicker, whisk in the optional arrowroot starch.

5. Serve the chicken with the reduced braising liquid and vegetables spooned on top.

fragrant spatchcocked
roasted chicken

serves 4 – 6

Spatchcocked may sound like a dirty word, but it's just a preparation technique that involves removing the backbone from a bird and pressing down on it so that it lies in one layer. This makes the chicken cook faster and more evenly—you get a perfectly roasted chicken in nearly half the time and with half the effort. This spatchcocked recipe has a bit of curry powder added for a slightly more extravagant taste that brings out the sweet, rich flavor of the moist, butter-basted chicken.

- 1 (3½–4 pound) chicken
- salt and pepper to taste
- 2 tablespoons softened butter or melted ghee, divided
- 1½ teaspoons curry powder
- 2 bunches sage
- 2 sprigs rosemary
- 4 cloves garlic

1. Preheat the oven to 425°F.

2. Rinse and pat dry the chicken, then place it on a cutting board breast side down. With kitchen shears, carefully cut from the neck down to the tail on both sides, and cut out the backbone. Flip the bird over so it's breast side up, then press firmly on the breast until you hear a crack and the chicken flattens. Tuck the wings back and salt and pepper the open part of the chicken. Rub 1 tablespoon of the softened butter or melted ghee all over the chicken, then sprinkle the curry powder evenly over the chicken and season with salt and pepper. Carefully pat down the seasonings a bit.

3. Place the sage, rosemary, and garlic on a rimmed baking sheet, and carefully lay the chicken on top, breast side up. Roast for 45 – 50 minutes or until the juices run clear when the chicken is pierced with a fork. Halfway through cooking, add the remaining 1 tablespoon butter in small pats or baste the remaining 1 tablespoon melted ghee all over the chicken.

4. Let the chicken rest for 10 minutes before carving and serving.

vinegar and shallot chicken

Since I began purchasing pastured chicken from my friends Jason and Lynsey at Yonder Way Farm, I have been able to appreciate the natural taste of the bird. Yonder Way's chickens are allowed to roam around and forage, which makes the meat's flavor much more pronounced and delightful as compared with flavorless, conventionally raised chicken. The ingredients in this recipe complement the chicken's natural flavor as if the combination were simply meant to be, with a light sweetness from the caramelized shallots and a large dose of umami from the combination of red wine vinegar and fish sauce. If I'm pressed for time or I forget about dinner until the last second, this is one of the recipes I turn to.

- 1 (3½–4 pound) chicken, cut into 8 pieces (breasts, thighs, legs, and wings)
- ¼ cup red wine vinegar
- 3 tablespoons avocado oil
- 1¼ tablespoons fish sauce
- 3–4 shallots (depending on size; see note), minced
- pepper to taste

1. Preheat the oven to 425°F. Rinse and pat dry the chicken.

2. In a medium-sized bowl, combine the red wine vinegar, avocado oil, fish sauce, and minced shallots and whisk until well combined. Season the chicken pieces with pepper and place them skin side up in a baking dish large enough to hold them in a single layer. Pour the liquid mixture over the chicken, toss to coat the chicken well, then flip the pieces so they're skin side down.

3. Cook for 20 minutes, then turn the chicken pieces over and cook for 25 more minutes or until the leg juices run clear when pierced with a fork. If you'd like to slightly crisp up and char some of the shallots on top, you can turn on the broiler for 3—4 minutes after the chicken is cooked through.

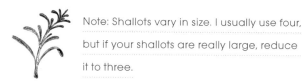

Note: Shallots vary in size. I usually use four, but if your shallots are really large, reduce it to three.

grilled coconut-basil chicken

serves 4—6

My friend Michelle Tam, author of the blog Nom Nom Paleo, has a couple of chicken recipes that involve puréeing a bunch of ingredients together to make a smooth paste in which to marinate the chicken, such as her sister's Grilled Green Chicken. After realizing how easy that method makes putting together a marinade and concentrating flavors, I decided to create my own "puréed marinade." Mine has some influences from Michelle's sister's recipe, with a zesty and umami-packed combination of flavors that gives grilled chicken an Asian twist.

- 4 cloves garlic
- 1 medium onion
- zest and juice of 1 lime
- 1 teaspoon coconut aminos or tamari
- 1 tablespoon fish sauce
- ½ cup coconut milk
- 6 large basil leaves
- ½ teaspoon pepper
- 1 (3½–4 pound) chicken, cut into 8 pieces (breasts, thighs, legs, and wings)
- 2 tablespoons ghee or avocado oil

1. In a blender, combine the garlic, onion, lime zest and juice, coconut aminos or tamari, fish sauce, coconut milk, basil, and pepper and purée until smooth.

2. Place the chicken pieces in a plastic bag and cover with the marinade. Refrigerate for at least 4 hours or overnight.

3. Preheat one side of a gas grill to high and the other side to low. When the grill is hot, grease the high-heat grates with the ghee or avocado oil. Grill the chicken pieces skin side down on the high-heat side for 6—10 minutes or until they easily pull from the grates and are charred to your liking. Flip the pieces and grill for 8 more minutes, then transfer them to the cool side of the grill, reduce the heat on the hot side of the grill to low, close the lid, and grill for 20 more minutes.

4. Let the chicken rest for at least 8 minutes before serving.

shredded chicken—cucumber bites

Once I needed a dish to bring to a neighborhood block party and was caught unprepared. I always bring some sort of food to a get-together, so this doesn't usually happen to me. A frantic search of the fridge brought me to a pair of cooked chicken breasts and a cucumber—thus the creation of this appetizer. It's not especially glamorous, but it went over quite well at the party. (Well, maybe I could have done better if I had known that half of our neighborhood doesn't like cucumber.) In this recipe, tender shredded chicken breast is mixed with a creamy and piquant barbecue sauce and mayonnaise dressing, then placed inside a thick slice of refreshing cucumber. These bites are excellent appetizers to bring to a party or eat as a quick lunch. Just make sure that whoever you're serving them to actually likes cucumber!

- 2 cooked chicken breasts (grilled, pan-cooked, roasted, etc.)
- ½ cup Mayonnaise (page 252)
- ⅓ cup Barbecue Sauce (page 249)
- 2 tablespoons chopped fresh chives, plus more for garnish
- ¼ teaspoon cayenne pepper
- salt and pepper to taste
- 1 large cucumber, cut into ½-inch slices
- ½ cup grape tomatoes, quartered

1. With 2 forks, shred the chicken into thick threads. In a medium-sized bowl, combine the shredded chicken, Mayonnaise, Barbecue Sauce, chives, cayenne pepper, and salt and pepper and mix well.

2. With a melon baller, scoop out the insides of the cucumber slices, making bowl shapes. Fill each cucumber "bowl" with the chicken mixture, top with a grape tomato quarter, and sprinkle with chopped chives.

Note: You can slow-cook the chicken breasts on low for 6 hours to make the chicken ahead of time.

chicken korma

My first attempt at making a curry was a chicken korma. Granted, I've made quite a few changes to my recipe since I first created it, but I didn't realize that I was making a korma-style curry until I looked it up. A korma-style curry is one of the better-known curries; it has a somewhat creamy and runny gravy that is mild in heat but rich in flavor. I use chicken legs and thighs rather than breasts for a more deeply flavored gravy that is sure to satisfy any hunger, especially one that yearns for Indian food like my brother's and mine.

- 2 teaspoons coriander seeds
- ¼ teaspoon cayenne pepper
- 1½ teaspoons garam masala
- ½ teaspoon ground cumin
- 4 chicken legs
- 4 chicken thighs
- salt and pepper to taste
- 3½ tablespoons ghee, divided
- 1 medium onion, chopped
- 4 cloves garlic, minced
- 2-inch knob of ginger, peeled and grated
- ¾ cup chicken Mother Stock (page 144)
- ½ cup plain full-fat yogurt or coconut milk
- 5 cardamom pods
- 1 cinnamon stick
- 2 bay leaves

1. In a small pan over medium heat, toast the coriander seeds until fragrant, about 3 minutes, shaking the pan to prevent burning. Pour the toasted coriander seeds into a mortar and pestle or spice grinder and grind until you have a fairly fine powder. In a small bowl, mix together the ground coriander, cayenne pepper, garam masala, and cumin.

2. Rinse and pat dry the chicken legs and thighs, then season with salt and pepper. Heat 2½ tablespoons of the ghee in a large Dutch oven or pot over medium-high heat, and brown the chicken in batches to prevent overcrowding, about 2—3 minutes per side. Place the browned pieces on a dish tented with foil.

3. Once all the chicken pieces are browned, reduce the heat to medium and add the remaining 1 tablespoon ghee to the pot. When the ghee is hot, stir in the onion, garlic, and ginger. Cook, stirring to prevent burning, until the onion is softened, about 2—3 minutes. Add the spice mixture and cook for about 30 seconds or until fragrant, stirring frequently to prevent burning, then add the chicken stock and yogurt or coconut milk while scraping the bottom of the pot. Bring to a light simmer, season with salt and pepper, then add the browned chicken pieces, accumulated juices in the dish, cardamom pods, cinnamon stick, and bay leaves.

4. Reduce the heat to low, cover, and cook for 40—45 minutes or until the juices from the legs run clear when pierced with a fork.

chicken leg quarters with caramelized spring onions and carrots

serves 4

I love all things caramelized; caramelization is nature's way of thanking you for your patience and care. In this recipe, chicken leg quarters are roasted in the oven untouched to let the fat slowly render and baste the spring onions and carrots until they are sweetened and perfectly caramelized.

- 2 bunches spring onions
- 3 carrots
- 5 cloves garlic, left in skins and smashed
- 6 sprigs marjoram
- ½ teaspoon fennel seeds
- ¼ cup red wine
- 2 tablespoons avocado oil, plus more for brushing on the chicken
- salt and pepper to taste
- 4 chicken leg quarters

1. Preheat the oven to 425°F.

2. In a roasting pan, scatter the onions, carrots, garlic cloves, marjoram, and fennel seeds. Pour in the red wine, drizzle the avocado oil over the veggies and around the pan, and season with salt and pepper.

3. Rinse and pat dry the chicken leg quarters, brush with avocado oil or melted ghee, and season with salt and pepper. Place the leg quarters on top of the vegetables in the roasting pan and roast for 45 minutes or until the juices run clear when pierced with a fork. Broil for an additional 2—4 minutes or until the chicken is browned to your liking.

slow cooker chicken with fennel and capers

I don't typically make food in a slow cooker because I enjoy the process of cooking something: smelling the scents that drift through the kitchen, peeking inside the cooking vessel, and tending to my upcoming meal. That said, an easy and satisfying meal without having to go out is always nice, especially when you're busy. Assemble the aromatics, place them in a slow cooker along with a whole chicken, and let it cook unattended. There is little work to do after it's done. Cooking doesn't get much easier than this, yet it comes out like a carefully tended-to meal.

- 1 (3½–4 pound) chicken
- 1 tablespoon avocado oil
- 1 lemon
- ½ teaspoon cayenne pepper
- 1 teaspoon paprika
- salt and pepper to taste
- 1 bulb fennel, cored and thinly sliced
- 5 cloves garlic, minced
- 3 medium leeks
- ½ cup white wine
- 2 tablespoons chopped fresh parsley

1. Rinse and pat dry the chicken, then coat it with the avocado oil. Zest the lemon, rub the zest all over the chicken, and season the chicken with the cayenne pepper, paprika, and salt and pepper. Cut the zested lemon into ¼-inch slices.

2. Cut off and discard the bottom root parts and the green hard parts of the leeks (or save them for making stock). Slice the remaining parts of the leeks in half lengthwise and then into slices about ⅓-inch thick. Place the sliced leeks in a medium-sized bowl, fill with water, and swish the water around to rinse off any dirt. Drain the water and pat the leeks dry with a paper towel.

3. In a slow cooker, add the fennel, garlic, lemon slices, leeks, and white wine. Season with salt and pepper and stir until well mixed. Place the chicken in the slow cooker on top of the vegetables, cover, and cook for 5–6 hours on low.

4. When the chicken is done, let it rest for 20 minutes, then separate the breasts, thighs, legs, and wings and broil for 4–5 minutes or until golden brown. Sprinkle the chopped parsley over the chicken and serve with the vegetables.

grilled citrus-mustard
split chicken breasts

serves 4

If I'm going to cook chicken breasts for a meal, I prefer them bone-in and skin-on because they stay moist and are far more flavorful than boneless, skinless breasts. Here, bone-in breasts are combined with a slightly sweet and tangy marinade, left to infuse, and then grilled. Boiling the marinade to use as a thick sauce for serving with the meat means that nothing is wasted.

- 2 tablespoons Dijon mustard
- 2 tablespoons whole-grain mustard
- 5 cloves garlic, minced
- 2 tablespoons avocado oil, plus more for brushing
- ¼ cup lemon juice
- 3 tablespoons orange juice
- 2½ teaspoons minced fresh rosemary
- 4 bone-in, skin-on chicken breasts
- ½ orange, cut into wedges
- ½ lemon, cut into wedges
- ¼ cup chopped fresh parsley

1. In a small bowl, combine the mustards, garlic, avocado oil, lemon juice, orange juice, and rosemary. Pour over the chicken breasts and marinate for at least 3 hours or overnight. Remove the chicken breasts from the marinade and pour the marinade into a small saucepan.

2. Preheat one side of a gas grill to high and the other side to low. Brush the hot-side grates with avocado oil. Grill the chicken breasts skin side down on the hot side for 7–9 minutes, moving them around until they are nicely charred, then flip and grill for 5 more minutes. Move the chicken to the cool side of the grill, reduce the heat on the hot side of the grill to low, close the lid, and grill for 15–20 minutes or until the chicken is golden brown.

3. While the chicken is cooking, bring the marinade to a boil in a small saucepan over medium-high heat. Reduce by about three-quarters or until the marinade is very thick.

4. Serve the chicken breasts brushed with the reduced marinade and garnished with orange and lemon wedges and parsley.

Note: There is no need to fear using the marinade as a sauce as long as it's cooked well before eating. Boiling the marinade will kill any bacteria that might have been in it.

crispy duck breasts with cherry-port sauce

Duck skin is prized by chefs and foodies around the world for two reasons: The fat underneath it has a unique and luxurious taste, and it becomes irresistibly crispy. Few things can beat perfectly crispy duck skin, especially on a plump and juicy duck breast. This recipe starts the duck breasts skin side down to let the fat render slowly and fry the skins, creating a beautifully crunchy and fatty shell to enrobe the duck breast. A slightly sweet and tart cherry-port sauce complements the richness of the fatty duck skin perfectly.

- 2 skin-on duck breasts
- salt and pepper to taste
- 1 tablespoon butter or ghee
- 1 shallot, minced
- 7 cherries, pitted and halved
- 2 tablespoons port
- 3 tablespoons chicken Mother Stock (page 144)
- 1 teaspoon balsamic vinegar

1. Rinse and pat dry the duck breasts. Use a sharp knife to score the skin in a crisscross pattern, being careful not to cut into the meat. Season the duck breasts on both sides with salt and pepper, then place in a room-temperature skillet on a turned-off burner. Turn the heat to low and cook the duck breasts for 5 minutes, then increase the heat to medium-low and cook for 10 more minutes. Increase the heat to medium and cook for 2 more minutes, then flip the duck breasts and cook for 5 more minutes. Remove the duck breasts from the pan and place on a cutting board to rest for at least 7 minutes.

2. While the duck breasts are resting, melt the butter or ghee in a small saucepan. Add the shallot and cherries and cook until the shallot is soft, about 3–4 minutes. Increase the heat to medium-high, add the port, let it bubble for a few seconds, then add the chicken stock and balsamic vinegar. Reduce the heat to medium and stir for 1–2 minutes.

3. Serve the whole duck breasts on a bed of sauce from the pan, or slice them and serve with the sauce drizzled on top.

Note: This recipe can easily be multiplied to serve more than two people; you just need to cook the duck breasts in multiple pans or one very large pan to avoid overcrowding.

bacon-wrapped dove breasts

My Uncle Larry knows his cuisine. He doesn't try too hard to make it look sophisticated all the time (his presentation is more rustic), but his dishes are always perfectly cooked and flavored. This recipe is my interpretation of one of his, a prized recipe among many hunters like himself. Tender dove breasts are stuffed with jalapeños to give them a slight sweetness with a little bit of heat, then wrapped up like beautiful parcels in smoky, salty bacon. The bacon wraps not only hold the dove breasts together but also baste them in bacon fat, keeping them from drying out and infusing them with a rich bacon flavor. Every time I think about them, I swoon.

- 10 strips bacon
- 3 jalapeños
- 10 dove breasts, sliced in half
- 1 tablespoon fresh oregano

1. Preheat a gas grill to medium heat.

2. Slice each strip of bacon and each jalapeño in half. Deseed the jalapeños, cut each half in half again, then slice each fourth in half widthwise to give you 8 pieces. Wrap each halved dove breast around a jalapeño piece and a little bit of oregano, then wrap with a bacon strip and secure with a toothpick.

3. Grill each bacon-wrapped dove breast for 8–10 minutes or until the bacon is cooked to your desired crispness, turning occasionally to ensure even cooking.

Note: Dove breasts can be difficult to acquire but can sometimes be found locally in areas where hunting is prevalent.

roasted turkey with bacon and rosemary gravy

serves 8—10

When I served this dish to my parents, their first words after tasting it were, "Please make this for Thanksgiving." I wholeheartedly agree that it's worthy of a special occasion, even though it can be made whenever you want. When roasting a turkey, it's important to do everything you can to keep it moist, especially the breast. I keep mine moist by stuffing the skin of the breast with a butter-herb mixture and then draping it in bacon. The bacon provides protection from overcooking and also bastes the turkey in its beautiful fat as it cooks. By the time the turkey is done, the bacon is fully cooked, crispy, and ready for use in the gravy. Once again, bacon proves itself to be the Swiss army knife of the kitchen.

- 2 cups water
- 1 (16–19 pound) turkey with separated neck
- salt and pepper to taste
- 2 large yellow onions, halved
- 2 bay leaves
- 2 lemons, divided
- 5 tablespoons unsalted butter, softened
- 3 cloves garlic, grated
- 3 tablespoons chopped fresh parsley
- 5 sage leaves, chopped finely
- 2 tablespoons avocado oil
- 6–7 strips bacon
- 4 sprigs rosemary, divided
- 1½ tablespoons apple cider vinegar

1. Preheat the oven to 450°F.

2. Bring the water to a boil in a medium-sized saucepan over medium-high heat. Add the turkey neck, cover, reduce the heat to low, place a diffuser over the burner if you have one, and let simmer. This will make a broth for use in the gravy.

3. Rinse and pat dry the turkey. Season the inside of the turkey with salt and pepper and stuff with the onions, bay leaves, and one of the lemons, halved.

4. In a small bowl, combine the softened butter, garlic, lemon zest and juice from the remaining lemon, parsley, sage, and salt and pepper and mix well. With your fingers, carefully loosen the breast skin, being careful not to tear it. Stuff the herb butter mixture under the breast skin and evenly distribute the mixture by pressing and rubbing the skin to move it around.

5. Season the outside of the turkey with salt and pepper, tuck the wings back, place in a roasting pan breast side up, and drizzle the breast with the avocado oil. Roast for 25 minutes, then remove from the oven and reduce the oven temperature to 350°F. Baste the turkey with the juices from the pan, then drape the bacon strips over the breast area to cover the entire breast. If you have any bacon strips left, drape them around the legs. Baste once more and then return to the oven for 2–2½ hours, basting occasionally, until an instant-read thermometer placed in the deepest part of the breast meat registers 160°F. Place the turkey on a serving tray and allow it to rest for 2 hours lightly tented with foil, making sure not to discard anything in the roasting pan.

6. After the turkey has rested, remove the thermometer and pour the juices that have accumulated in the bottom of the serving tray into a small bowl. Remove the lemon halves from

the cavity and set them aside. Remove the onions from the cavity and the bacon from the breast and place on a cutting board. Place the roasting pan on the stovetop over medium heat. Cut the stems off the onions and chop the onions and bacon. Add the chopped bacon and onions to the roasting pan along with 3 of the rosemary sprigs and stir. Remove the wing tips and tail from the turkey and add to the roasting pan. Stir and allow the flavors to intensify for 2 minutes. Turn the heat off the turkey neck broth, pour all the liquid along with the neck and the apple cider vinegar into the roasting pan, and stir. Squeeze in the juice of the lemon halves from the cavity, season lightly with salt and pepper, and simmer for 2—3 minutes or until very fragrant, making sure not to let it reduce too much. Turn off the heat and remove the rosemary sprigs, wing tips, tail, and neck. Pour everything remaining into a blender and purée until smooth. Pour the gravy into a gravy boat or small serving bowl, add the remaining sprig of rosemary, and let it infuse for 5 minutes.

7. Carve the turkey, remove the rosemary sprig from the gravy, and serve.

Note: This recipe is quite flexible when it comes to the weight of the turkey; you can use a smaller or larger bird. Just be aware that the cooking time will be shorter or longer depending on the weight. Be sure to keep an eye on your thermometer, and pull the turkey out of the oven when it reaches 160°F. I highly recommend using an electronic thermometer that you can leave in the turkey the whole time to monitor the temperature continuously.

—— meat ——

steak and brussels sprouts stir-fry

A stir-fry is typically prepared very quickly while shaking the pan frequently, making it perfect for a fast and easy weeknight meal. I enjoy pretty much any stir-fry, but this recipe combines two of my favorite things to put on a plate: steak and Brussels sprouts. Call me weird, but I love a steak that is wonderfully charred on the outside and pink on the inside with Brussels sprouts on the side. Making a stir-fry out of them gets them onto my plate twice as fast, and with an Asian flair to boot.

- 3½ tablespoons ghee, divided
- 12 ounces Brussels sprouts, stems trimmed, cut into fourths
- salt and pepper to taste
- 2-inch knob of ginger, peeled and minced
- 1 teaspoon sesame oil
- 2 teaspoons fish sauce
- 1 tablespoon coconut aminos or tamari
- 2 tablespoons unseasoned rice vinegar
- 3 cloves garlic, minced
- 1½ pounds sirloin steak, thinly sliced
- 2 Thai red chile peppers, thinly sliced
- 3 green onions, thinly sliced, whites minced
- 1 large carrot, shaved into thin ribbons with a vegetable peeler

1. Heat 1 tablespoon of the ghee in a large pan or wok over medium-high heat. Add the Brussels sprouts, immediately lower the heat to medium-low, and season with salt and pepper. Cover the pan with a lid or foil and cook for 3 minutes, then shake the pan, increase the heat to medium, cover, and cook for 2 more minutes.

2. Remove the cooked Brussels sprouts to a plate. In a small bowl, combine the ginger, sesame oil, fish sauce, coconut aminos or tamari, rice vinegar, and garlic. Wipe out the pan or wok, then heat the remaining 2½ tablespoons ghee over high heat. Add the steak and sear for 2 minutes, then shake the pan and cook for another 2 minutes. Reduce the heat to medium-high and add the sauce mixture along with the chile peppers, green onions, and shaved carrot, shaking the pan and stirring often to thoroughly incorporate the ingredients. Return the cooked Brussels sprouts to the pan with the beef and continue cooking for 2 more minutes, shaking the pan and stirring frequently. Serve immediately.

Notes: Make sure that your rice vinegar is unseasoned. Seasoned rice vinegar contains additives like sugar and sometimes preservatives.

I typically serve this dish with cauliflower rice, as pictured. It is made in a similar way to Fragrant Indian Cauliflower "Couscous" (page 172), pulsed in a food processor but left a little chunkier and without all the extra spices—only cauliflower, salt, and pepper.

red wine—braised short ribs with rosemary, thyme, and black trumpets

serves 3—4

This recipe is one of my absolute favorites. These short ribs are fairly easy to prepare, yet incredibly decadent and sophisticated. There isn't much to do except to slowly simmer the ribs in a Dutch oven and let the flavors meld, creating a rich, silky sauce to complement the deliciously caramelized, fork-tender, and delicate meat. The wonderful thing about this recipe is the awe factor it creates when you serve it, making it perfect for a get-together—and you can make it ahead of time.

- ½ ounce dried black trumpet mushrooms
- 1 cup water
- 3–4 strips bacon
- 2–3 pounds beef short ribs
- salt and pepper to taste
- 2½–3 tablespoons ghee or avocado oil, divided
- 1 medium onion, coarsely chopped
- 1 medium carrot, coarsely chopped
- 1 stalk celery, cut into ¼-inch slices
- 1 tablespoon tomato paste
- 2½ cups red wine
- 4 sprigs rosemary
- 3 large sprigs thyme

1. Place the dried black trumpet mushrooms in a small bowl. Heat the water until it's hot but not boiling, then pour the hot water over the mushrooms. Let soak for 25 minutes. While the mushrooms are soaking, preheat the oven to 325°F.

2. Once the mushrooms have soaked, squeeze out any excess liquid over the bowl in which you soaked them, and reserve the soaking liquid. Chop the mushrooms coarsely and set aside. Chop the bacon widthwise into ½-inch slices.

3. If your short ribs are a whole section with several ribs, cut evenly between the ribs to give you individual cuts. Season each short rib with salt and pepper.

4. Heat a large Dutch oven over medium heat. Add the chopped bacon and fry until crispy. Remove the bacon, but leave the fat in the Dutch oven. Add 1½–2 tablespoons of the avocado oil or ghee, depending on the amount of bacon fat in the pan; you want just enough to coat the entire bottom. Increase the heat to medium-high, add the short ribs in batches, keeping them from overcrowding, and brown well on all sides, about 1—2 minutes per side. Place the browned short ribs in a bowl or dish tented with foil.

5. When all the short ribs are nicely browned on all sides, add the remaining 1 tablespoon avocado oil or ghee, reduce the heat to medium, add the soaked black trumpet mushrooms, and sauté for 1—2 minutes. Add the onion, carrot, celery, and tomato paste and cook for another 2—3 minutes, stirring often to prevent burning. Once the onion begins to soften, pour in the red wine and the reserved soaking liquid from the mushrooms, scraping any bits stuck to the bottom of the Dutch oven to deglaze it. Add a pinch of salt and pepper and continue stirring. Let the mixture come to a light simmer, then reduce the heat to low and place the browned short ribs back in the pot, spaced evenly. Nestle the rosemary and thyme sprigs all around the meat, then sprinkle in the bacon.

Note: As with most braises, this dish is much better the next day. The extra time allows the flavors to marry, and the fat hardens in the fridge, which makes it much easier to defat. Not to mention that it is incredibly easy for quick serving when you have guests. Make the ribs ahead of time, let them cool, and refrigerate covered with foil. Then all you have to do is reheat them in a 375°F oven until hot and bubbly and serve.

6. Cover and place in the oven for 2½–3 hours or until the meat is fork-tender. Check the braise halfway through cooking to make sure that it isn't simmering too hard. If it is, lower the oven temperature to 315°F and continue braising.

7. When the ribs are done, place the meat on a warmed dish tented with foil and set aside. With a spoon, carefully remove the rosemary and thyme sprigs. Defat the braising liquid by pressing your spoon flat over the liquid and slowly letting the fat (but not the broth) run into the spoon. Do not completely defat the liquid; you just want to remove the pool of fat that has developed. Place the Dutch oven on the stovetop over medium heat and reduce the braising liquid by a third.

8. Serve with the braising liquid and vegetables spooned over the short ribs.

cacao oven brisket

The best way to make a brisket, hands down, is to cook it for an immensely long time in a smoker, with meticulous care. Sadly, not everyone has a smoker or the time to watch over it for hours. I managed to pull together a brisket that can be made in the oven without having to be checked frequently. You still get the incredibly tender, smoky, and juicy meat that you would in a smoker.

for the spice rub:

- 1 tablespoon unsweetened cacao powder
- 1½ teaspoons garlic powder
- 1 teaspoon chili powder
- 1 teaspoon mustard powder
- ½ teaspoon onion powder
- ½ teaspoon cinnamon
- ½ teaspoon pepper
- 1 teaspoon salt
- ¼ teaspoon cayenne pepper

- 3–4 pounds beef brisket
- 1 tablespoon liquid smoke

1. Preheat the oven to 250°F.

2. In a small bowl, combine the spice rub ingredients. Cover the brisket with the liquid smoke, then rub it all over with the spice rub.

3. Place a wire rack in the bottom of a roasting pan, then place the spice-rubbed brisket on the rack. Cover the roasting pan tightly with foil and cook for 6—7 hours, depending on the size of your brisket.

4. Uncover and place under the broiler for 3 minutes. Remove from the oven and allow to rest, lightly tented with foil, for at least 25 minutes before slicing and serving.

Note: Watch out for fake liquid smoke that is made with artificial ingredients and/or sugar. The brand I use, Wrights Liquid Smoke, is made of nothing but smoke from hickory wood that is filtered into water.

sweet rosemary meatballs

serves 2—3

I had just gotten home with some incredibly vibrant carrots that had been picked that day, and I couldn't contain my excitement; I had to use them in something while they were so fresh! I chopped up the biggest one in the bunch and put it in some meatballs. To my surprise, it gave the meatballs a wonderfully nuanced texture along with a massive addition of flavor.

- 1 pound ground beef
- 1 shallot, minced
- 3 cloves garlic, minced
- 1 large carrot, chopped into small chunks
- 2 tablespoons minced fresh rosemary
- salt and pepper to taste
- 1 egg
- 1 tablespoon lard or ghee

1. In a medium-sized bowl, combine the ground beef, shallot, garlic, carrot, rosemary, and salt and pepper. In a separate, smaller bowl, whisk the egg. Pour the egg into the meat mixture and mix thoroughly with your hands or a fork. Form the mixture into 2-inch meatballs.

2. Heat the lard or ghee in a large pan over medium-high heat. When the pan is hot, add the meatballs, evenly spaced, and sear for 3—5 minutes. Turn the meatballs to brown all sides, about 2—3 minutes per side. The meatballs are done when they have a little bit of spring left to them and are no longer mushy when lightly squeezed.

avocado-stuffed chile-lime burgers with grilled spring onions

serves 2—3

Burgers are always a fast and delicious meal, but they can get boring. To keep things interesting, I stuff my burgers with various things. My absolute favorite stuffing is avocado. A fresh, creamy surprise awaits as you bite into this burger, which is spiced with smoky chipotle chili powder and zesty lime and topped with a charred spring onion.

- 1 egg
- 1 pound ground beef
- ¼ teaspoon pepper
- 1 teaspoon chipotle chili powder
- ¼ teaspoon smoked paprika
- ½ teaspoon salt, plus more to taste
- zest and juice of 1 lime, divided
- 1 large avocado
- 1 bunch spring onions or green onions
- melted ghee or avocado oil for brushing

1. Preheat a gas grill to medium-high heat. In a small bowl, whisk the egg. In a medium-sized bowl, add the ground beef, pepper, chipotle chili powder, smoked paprika, ½ teaspoon salt, lime zest, and whisked egg and mix until thoroughly incorporated.

2. In another small bowl, mash the avocado with the lime juice and salt to taste until smooth.

3. Form the meat into 2—3 patties, then split the patties in half and flatten them (they will be thin, but don't worry; you will be placing the other half on top to re-form the burgers). Take one of the flattened halves, add a dollop of the avocado mixture, place another half on top, and pinch the edges shut to seal. Repeat with the remaining halves until all the burgers are stuffed.

4. Brush the spring onions with melted ghee or avocado oil. Grease the grates on the hot side of the grill lightly with ghee or avocado oil and add the stuffed burgers and spring onions, spacing everything apart. Grill for 3—4 minutes, flipping the spring onions occasionally, then flip the burgers and grill for another 3 minutes. Close the lid and cook for 2 more minutes, then serve with the grilled spring onions.

slow-roasted lamb shoulder
with parsley sauce

serves 6 — 8

Lamb's unique flavor is sadly overlooked by many people. The frequency with which people tell me that they have never had lamb or don't like lamb shocks me. Slow-roasting a lamb shoulder with a bit of garlic, rosemary, and a subtle hint of sweet cinnamon lets its delicate flavor shine, while the meat becomes beautifully succulent and ridiculously tender. Not to mention that this recipe is as easy as scoring a piece of lamb, placing it in a roasting pan with some herbs, tenting it with foil, and then popping it into the oven and walking away. The only catch is that you must remember to come back when it's done.

- 3–4 pounds lamb shoulder, boneless or bone-in
- 7 cloves garlic, divided
- 7 sprigs rosemary, divided
- 1 cinnamon stick (optional)
- 2 tablespoons avocado oil or melted ghee
- salt and pepper to taste
- ½ cup chicken Mother Stock (page 144)
- 2 tablespoon red wine vinegar
- juice of ½ lemon
- ¼ cup lightly packed fresh parsley
- 2 tablespoons capers

1. Preheat the oven to 325°F.

2. Place the lamb shoulder fat side up on a cutting board and use a sharp knife to score the entire fat cap in a crisscross pattern.

3. In a roasting pan or Dutch oven, arrange 3 cloves of the garlic, 4 sprigs of the rosemary, and the cinnamon stick, if using. Place the lamb on top, fat side up. Place the remaining garlic and rosemary on top of the lamb, then drizzle the lamb with the avocado oil or melted ghee and season generously with salt and pepper. Cover the pan tightly with foil and roast for 4 hours.

4. Take the roasting pan out of the oven and remove the foil. If you want a crispier top, put it back in the oven with the foil off and broil on high for 3—5 minutes.

5. Remove the lamb from the roasting pan and lightly tent with foil to keep warm. Remove the garlic, rosemary, and cinnamon stick and reserve the garlic. Pour the rendered lamb fat out of the roasting pan and refrigerate for another use or discard. Place the roasting pan on the stovetop over medium heat and pour in the chicken stock and red wine vinegar, scraping all the sticky bits from the bottom of the pan. Squeeze in the reserved roasted garlic cloves. Chop the parsley and capers together so that they are well incorporated, add to the pan, and stir. Simmer for 4 minutes.

6. Cut the lamb into chunks or simply plate with a large fork, and serve with some of the sauce spooned over the top.

lamb shanks braised in coffee and ancho chile

serves 4

Lamb shank is one of my favorite cuts of lamb, but transforming the tough connective tissue–filled meat to melt-in-your-mouth tenderness requires a little bit of patience and cooking time. A classic way to cook lamb shanks is to braise them in a flavorful liquid like broth or tomato sauce. This recipe uses smoky coffee and slightly sweet and peppery ancho chiles instead. The flavor profile is somewhat atypical, but I think that might change in a hurry; I can't think of a better way to prepare lamb shanks than with a slow braise in this powerfully flavored liquid.

- 2 teaspoons coriander seeds
- ½ teaspoon fennel seeds
- 4 lamb shanks (about 1 pound each)
- 3½ tablespoons ghee or avocado oil, divided
- salt and pepper to taste
- 1 large yellow onion, chopped
- 5 cloves garlic, minced
- 1 jalapeño, seeded and cut into ¼-inch slices
- 1¼ tablespoons ancho chile powder
- ¾ cup crushed tomatoes (you can use canned; just watch out for BPA linings)
- 1 cup strong brewed coffee
- 2 cups beef Mother Stock (page 144)
- 2 tablespoons red wine vinegar

Note: Depending on how deep your pot or Dutch oven is, you may want to place parchment paper between the lid and the pot to create a tighter seal. This is necessary only if the pot is filled less than halfway.

1. Preheat the oven to 350°F.

2. In a small skillet over medium heat, toast the coriander seeds for 2–3 minutes or until fragrant, shaking the pan often to prevent burning. Place the toasted coriander seeds and the fennel seeds in a mortar and pestle or spice grinder and grind until you have a fine powder.

3. Wash and pat dry the lamb shanks. They may have a thin white membrane known as silver skin around them; remove that by carefully inserting the tip of a sharp knife under it, carefully cutting an opening in it, and peeling it off. You may need to cut around it, as some are tougher than others; just be careful not to pierce the meat underneath.

4. Heat 2½ tablespoons of the ghee or avocado oil in a large oven-safe pot or Dutch oven over medium-high heat. When it's hot, season the lamb shanks with salt and pepper and brown them in batches, 2–3 minutes per side. Place the browned shanks on a platter tented with foil. Once all the shanks are browned, pour out any remaining cooking fat, and pat the bottom of the pot with a paper towel.

5. Place the pot back on the burner and heat the remaining 1 tablespoon ghee or avocado oil over medium heat. Stir in the onion, garlic, and jalapeño and cook until softened, about 2–3 minutes. Add the ground coriander and fennel seeds and ancho chile powder and cook, stirring often to prevent burning, for about 30 seconds or until very fragrant. Pour in the crushed tomatoes, coffee, and beef stock, scraping the bottom of the pot with a wooden spoon, then add the red wine vinegar, season with salt and pepper, and stir.

6. Bring the braising liquid to a simmer and place the browned lamb shanks in the liquid, arranging them so that each shank is submerged. Pour any accumulated juices from the platter over the shanks. Cover and place in the preheated oven for 2½–3 hours or until the meat pulls easily from the bone. After about 20 minutes of braising, check the shanks. If they are simmering too hard, reduce the oven temperature by 20–30°F for the remainder of the braising time.

7. Defat the braising liquid slightly. Serve with the braising liquid and vegetables spooned over the lamb shanks.

lamb vindaloo

Of all the meats, I feel that lamb accompanies the flavors of a curry best. According to my mom, this is one of the best curries I've ever made, and I tend to agree. The rich, tender lamb shoulder is slowly simmered in a fragrant and deeply flavored gravy until it's fork-tender. As with any curry, the gravy is the most important part; letting this one thicken in the last 15 minutes or so intensifies the flavors so that you can taste each and every spice in perfect unison.

for the spice paste:

- 2-inch knob of ginger, peeled
- 8 cloves garlic
- ½ cup white wine vinegar
- 1 tablespoon tomato paste
- ¾–1½ teaspoons cayenne pepper
- 1½ teaspoons paprika
- ½ teaspoon ground cumin
- ½ teaspoon mustard powder
- 4 whole cloves

- 3 tablespoons ghee, divided
- 3 pounds boneless lamb shoulder, cut into 1- to 2-inch chunks
- salt and pepper to taste
- 1 large onion, finely chopped
- ½ cup chicken Mother Stock (page 144)
- 1 cinnamon stick

1. Place all the ingredients for the spice paste in a blender or food processor and process until completely smooth.

2. In a large pot or Dutch oven, heat 2 tablespoons of the ghee over high heat. Season the lamb with salt and pepper, then brown in batches to avoid overcrowding the pan, placing each batch on a tray to accumulate juices as you brown. Once all the lamb is browned, reduce the heat to medium and add the remaining 1 tablespoon ghee to the pot. When the ghee is hot, add the onion and cook until softened, about 2—3 minutes. Add the spice paste and stir frequently to prevent burning for 30 seconds to 1 minute, then add the chicken stock while scraping the bottom of the pot. Add the browned lamb along with the accumulated juices from the tray and the cinnamon stick. Season generously with salt and pepper, reduce the heat to low, and cook, covered, for 2½ hours.

3. Remove the lid, increase the heat to medium-low, and simmer, uncovered, stirring often, for 15 minutes or until very reduced and thickened.

Note: A classic lamb vindaloo is quite spicy, but feel free to reduce the amount of cayenne pepper if you fear that it will be too spicy for your taste. Because I like it at least tolerably spicy, I don't go above 1½ teaspoons, although it's fairly spicy even then. I think that most people can handle ¾ teaspoon cayenne pepper, which gives it a nice warm heat that isn't overpowering but is definitely noticeable. At ¾ teaspoon, my friend Jason from Yonder Way Farm rated it a 5 on a spiciness scale of 1 to 10.

————— meat —————

rosemary and coriander crusted
rack of lamb

serves 2

As Gordon Ramsay once said, "Rack of lamb is like the Rolls-Royce of lamb." I completely agree, so I added some spices and mustard to complement the lamb rather than mask its flavor. The wonderful thing about adding the mustard after the lamb is browned is that it instantly melts into the tender fat of the lamb, lightly flavoring the whole rack inside and out. This recipe takes less than 30 minutes to prepare, yet it yields a cut of meat that's more flavorful and tender than beef tenderloin.

- 1 rack of lamb (about 1¼ pounds)
- ¼ cup fresh rosemary
- 1 tablespoon coriander seeds
- ½ tablespoon fresh thyme
- salt and pepper to taste
- 2 tablespoons ghee
- 1 tablespoon whole-grain mustard
- 4 cloves garlic, left in skins and smashed

1. Preheat the oven to 450°F.

2. Rinse and pat dry the rack of lamb, then use a sharp knife to score the entire fat cap in a crisscross pattern, being careful not to cut into the meat.

3. Place the rosemary, coriander seeds, thyme, and salt and pepper in a food processor or blender and process until coarsely ground and well incorporated.

4. Heat the ghee in a large pan or cast-iron skillet over medium-high heat. When the ghee is hot, brown the lamb for 2—3 minutes on each side, then turn off the heat. Place the lamb on a cutting board, brush with the mustard, and pat with the herb mixture. Place the crusted rack of lamb fat cap side down in the same pan along with the smashed garlic cloves and roast in the oven for 7—8 minutes for medium-rare. Transfer the lamb to a cutting board and let it rest, lightly tented with foil, for 8—10 minutes before slicing and serving.

Note: This recipe can easily be multiplied to serve more people; just brown the racks of lamb individually so as not to overcrowd the pan. Then continue the recipe normally, keeping the racks of lamb spaced far enough apart that they don't touch each other.

osso bucco with gremolata

Osso bucco is one of those classics that many people know the name of but surprisingly don't know how to cook. This is a fairly traditional recipe, but I put my own spin on it. The veal shanks are braised to melt-in-your-mouth tenderness in a vibrant white wine and herb cooking liquid, along with the classic aromatic combination of carrot, onion, and celery known as a mirepoix, and finished with a refreshing gremolata to cut the richness. It is truly a recipe that everyone should have in his or her repertoire.

- 3½ tablespoons ghee, divided
- 4 cross-cut meaty veal shanks (about 3–3½ pounds total)
- 1 medium onion, coarsely chopped
- 3 cloves garlic, minced
- ½ bulb fennel, coarsely chopped
- 1 carrot, coarsely chopped
- 1 stalk celery, coarsely chopped
- 1 teaspoon chopped fresh thyme
- 1½ teaspoons chopped fresh marjoram
- 1 cup white wine
- ½ cup veal stock or chicken Mother Stock (page 144)
- ½ cup peeled and chopped tomatoes (fresh or canned)
- 1 bay leaf

for the gremolata:

- 2 tablespoons chopped fresh parsley
- 1 teaspoon minced garlic
- 1½ teaspoons lemon zest (about 1 lemon, zested)

1. Preheat the oven to 300°F.

2. In a large Dutch oven or pot, heat 2½ tablespoons of the ghee over medium-high heat, then brown the veal shanks in batches to avoid overcrowding the pot, 3–4 minutes per side. Place the browned pieces on a tray tented with foil. Once all the shanks are browned, reduce the heat to medium, carefully dab the pan dry with a paper towel, then add the remaining 1 tablespoon ghee. Add the onion, garlic, fennel, carrot, celery, thyme, and marjoram. Cook until the onion is softened, about 2–3 minutes, then pour in the white wine, veal or chicken stock, and chopped tomatoes, scraping the bottom of the pot. Bring to a light simmer, add the shanks back to the pot along with the bay leaf, and reduce the heat to low. Cover the pot with parchment paper to create a tighter seal, then cover with the lid. Place in the preheated oven for 2–2½ hours or until the meat pulls easily from the bone. Remove the lid and parchment paper and broil for 3 minutes on high, then remove from the oven.

3. Combine all the ingredients for the gremolata and serve the osso bucco with a sprinkle of gremolata on top.

 Note: This dish goes great with plain cauliflower mash. Make it using my Loaded Cauliflower Mash recipe (page 216), but omit the bacon, chives, and cheese. Or leave them in—there's nothing wrong with having osso bucco on top of a loaded cauliflower mash. It just happens to be quite rich on its own.

pan-roasted spiced pork chops
with lemon and sage

serves 4

When cut and prepared properly, pork chops are among my favorite cuts of the pig. I always judge a pork chop by the fat cap. You want at least a 1-inch fat cap because it keeps the pork moist and flavorful. The only downside of a fat cap is that the chop tends to curl the second it hits a hot pan—which is why I like to score the fat cap all the way down the chop so that it refrains from curling and browns evenly to create a nice dark crust. Not to mention that the fat cap renders faster and quite a bit more when scored, so the chop gets the chance to sit in its fat and gather all that intense flavor while the fat cap gets nice and crispy.

- 4 (1-inch-thick) pork chops, preferably bone-in
- 1 lemon, halved
- 2 teaspoons ground cumin
- 1 teaspoon coriander
- ½ teaspoon salt
- ½ teaspoon pepper
- 2 tablespoons ghee or bacon fat
- 6 sage leaves
- 5 cloves garlic, left in skins and smashed

1. Preheat the oven to 350°F. Cut one of the lemon halves into wedges for serving later.

2. Rinse and pat dry the pork chops. With kitchen shears or a sharp knife, score the fat cap by cutting along the cap at ½-inch intervals.

3. In a small dish, combine the cumin, coriander, salt, and pepper. Divide the spice mixture evenly among the 4 pork chops and rub it on both sides of each chop.

4. In an oven-safe pan large enough to hold all the pork chops without overcrowding, heat the ghee or bacon fat over medium-high heat. When the fat is hot, place the spice-rubbed chops in the pan and sear for 2—3 minutes, then flip and sear for another minute.

5. After the pork chops have been seared, hold one chop fat cap side down at an edge of the pan. Tilt the pan in that direction for 15—20 seconds to let the cooking fat slightly render and crisp up the fat cap, then lay it back down on the side that was most recently on the pan. Repeat this process for each chop.

6. Add the sage and garlic to the pan, squeeze the juice of the other lemon half over the pork chops, and place the pan in the preheated oven for 10 minutes.

7. When the pork chops are done, place on a warmed dish and let rest for at least 5 minutes. Dredge the chops in the leftover pan juices and serve with the lemon wedges.

pulled pork with spicy vinegar sauce

When it comes to making pulled pork, I prefer to do it slowly in the oven rather than in a slow cooker. I feel like I have a lot less control with a slow cooker, plus I like the more interactive and intimate process of cooking something in the oven: you get to check on it and control the steps in order to coax the dish into perfection. To my pulled pork, I add a spicy vinegar sauce that is much like a North Carolina–style barbecue sauce. The vinegar base wakes up the flavor of the pork and adds a subtle tart-sweetness, while the red pepper flakes give it just a touch of heat.

for the spice mix:

- 2 teaspoons paprika
- 1 teaspoon ground cumin
- 2 teaspoons onion powder
- 1½ teaspoons garlic powder
- 1 teaspoon chipotle chili powder
- ½ teaspoon pepper
- 1 teaspoon salt
- 1 teaspoon cinnamon

- 3–6 pounds bone-in pork shoulder or Boston butt

for the spicy vinegar sauce:

- ⅓ cup apple cider vinegar
- 1 tablespoon tomato paste
- ¼ teaspoon red pepper flakes
- ¼ teaspoon salt
- ½ teaspoon pepper
- 1 teaspoon honey or 3 drops liquid stevia (optional)

1. Preheat the oven to 300°F.

2. In a small bowl, combine all the spice mix ingredients, then rub the spice mix all over the pork shoulder. Roast for 6—8 hours or until the pork reaches an internal temperature of 195°F.

3. Allow the pork to cool slightly. While the pork is cooling, mix together the ingredients for the spicy vinegar sauce in another small bowl.

4. When the pork is cool enough to handle, shred it with 2 forks, pour the sauce over the pork, and toss well.

5. Serve in lettuce cups or on Cauliflower Tortillas (see my recipe on page 208).

herbed pork loin

In my opinion, a boneless pork loin calls for stuffing—specifically a stuffing of vibrant lemon zest and fragrant sage. I prefer my pork loin at the very least with a fat cap, but preferably with the skin on, too. Leaving the fat cap or skin on gives you a nice crispy crust around each slice of pork. Scoring the fat or skin and giving the loin a decent coating of oil before you roast it helps the scored section render faster, making it crisp and succulent when it comes out of the oven. The best part is that you get a beautiful and deeply flavored rolled, stuffed, and crispy-edged pork loin after only 45 minutes in the oven.

- 3–4 pounds boneless pork loin, with at least a ½-inch fat cap or skin-on

- 1 lemon

- 10–15 sage leaves

- 4 sprigs parsley

- 1 teaspoon chopped fresh thyme

- 3 cloves garlic, thinly sliced

- 3 tablespoons crumbled goat cheese (optional)

- 2 tablespoons avocado oil, divided

- salt and pepper to taste

- kitchen twine

1. Preheat the oven to 425°F and line a baking sheet with foil.

2. Rinse and pat dry the pork loin. Use a sharp knife to score the fat cap or skin in a crisscross pattern, being careful not to cut into the meat, then flip it over so that the fat cap is facedown. Using a long, sharp knife and starting 1 inch above the fat cap, slowly slice the pork loin lengthwise, carefully opening it like a book until it lays flat, being careful not to slice all the way through.

3. Zest the lemon over the entire open surface of the pork loin. Cover one side with the sage leaves, then cover the opposite side with the parsley and thyme. Evenly distribute the sliced garlic and goat cheese, if using, over the herbs and lemon zest, then drizzle ½ tablespoon of the avocado oil over the herb and garlic mixture and season with salt and pepper. Carefully reroll the pork loin, fat side up, and secure with kitchen twine, tying simple knots at 1-inch intervals.

4. Place the pork loin fat side up on the foil-lined baking sheet. Season liberally with salt and pepper, then drizzle it with the remaining 1½ tablespoons avocado oil. With the bottom side of the rolled pork loin, dab up any salt, pepper, or avocado oil that landed on the baking sheet.

5. Roast the pork loin for 45 minutes, then pull it out of the oven and let it rest for 15 minutes before serving. If it isn't browned enough, broil on high for 2—3 minutes to crisp up the top.

Note: If you're making this dish with a skin-on pork loin, you will probably need to take it out of the oven when it's done, turn up the heat to 500 degrees, and then place it back in the oven until the skin is crisp and puffed.

shepherd's pie

My mom is the one who introduced me to British food, which is odd because she's a Texan. I suppose it's because both cultures have similar standards when it comes to comfort food. One of her favorite British dishes is shepherd's pie, which is typically made with ground lamb or beef and various aromatics, topped with mashed potatoes and a sprinkle of cheese, and lightly browned in the oven. To make my shepherd's pie even more healthful and surprisingly delicious, I use cauliflower puree in place of potatoes. While I'm an advocate of real food and don't mind eating a white potato, I think the cauliflower puree makes this shepherd's pie a little better and more interesting; its sweetness complements the hearty meat mixture and tomato wonderfully.

- 1½ heads cauliflower, trimmed and cut into uniform florets
- 1 tablespoon butter
- 1 egg yolk
- salt and pepper to taste
- 1½ tablespoons ghee
- 1 medium yellow onion, finely chopped
- 1 large carrot, finely chopped
- 1 stalk celery, finely chopped
- 2 cloves garlic, thinly sliced
- 1 pound ground bison
- 1 pound ground pork
- ¼ cup beef Mother Stock (page 144)
- ½ cup crushed tomatoes
- 1½ teaspoons chopped fresh thyme
- ¾ cup grated Parmesan cheese (optional)

Note: The Parmesan is optional, but without it, the browning won't be as nice-looking. You can substitute ground beef if you don't have ground bison; the flavor will just be slightly different.

1. Preheat the oven to 400°F.

2. If you have a pressure cooker, place the cauliflower florets in an elevated steamer basket and cook at high pressure for 4 minutes, then release the pressure by using the quick-release method. If you don't have a pressure cooker, steam the florets in a steamer basket over boiling water for 10 minutes or until soft.

3. Add the steamed cauliflower, butter, and egg yolk to a blender or food processor, season with salt, and process until smooth.

4. In a large skillet, heat the ghee over medium heat. Add the onion, carrot, celery, and garlic and cook for 3—4 minutes or until the onion is softened. Add the ground meats, turn the heat to high, and cook for 3—4 minutes, stirring often, until the meat is thoroughly browned. Lower the heat to medium, add the beef stock, crushed tomatoes, and thyme, season with salt and pepper, and stir. Simmer for 8—10 minutes or until the liquid has evaporated.

5. Pour the meat mixture into a baking dish or casserole. Cover the meat with the cauliflower puree, sprinkle the Parmesan (if using) over the top, and lightly fork the puree to create peaks without penetrating past the cauliflower. Bake for 40—45 minutes or until it begins to bubble and brown. If it's not browned to your liking, broil it on high for 2—3 minutes.

6. Allow the shepherd's pie to cool for at least 7 minutes before serving.

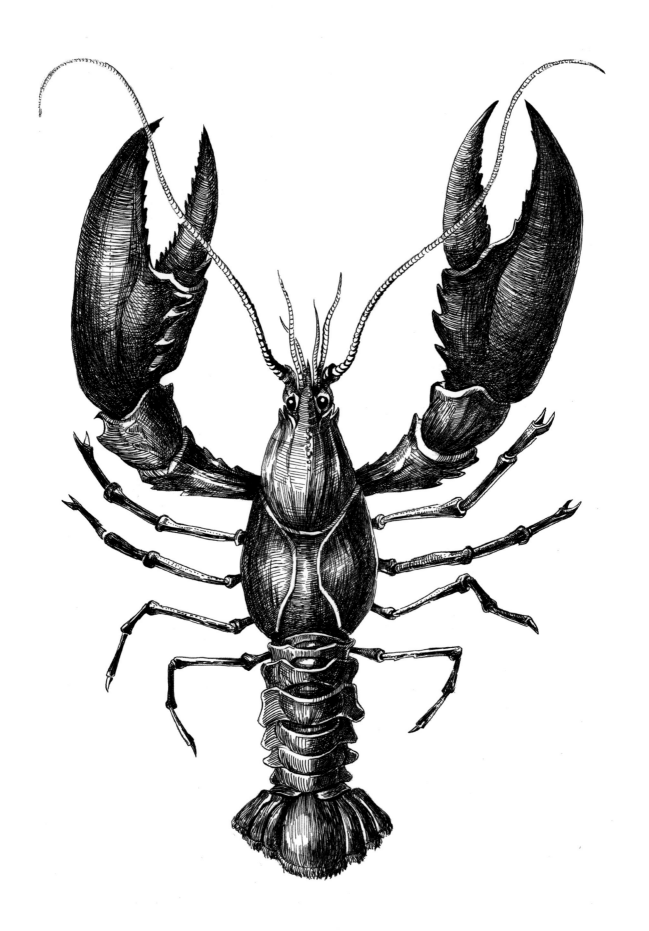

———— seafood ————

braised halibut with creamed leeks

Halibut is one of my favorite types of fish. Its subtle yet distinct flavor goes well with almost anything because it's so light. I enjoy halibut with something acidic on it and a fresh side, but sometimes you need to counteract the lightness of a fish or meat by introducing some rich elements. In this recipe, soft-fleshed halibut is immersed in a thick and creamy concoction of sweet and subtle leeks and fruity white wine and braised to tender, moist perfection.

- 3 medium leeks
- 3 tablespoons butter or ghee
- 4 cloves garlic, minced
- salt and pepper to taste
- ¾ cup white wine
- 1½ tablespoons chopped fresh thyme
- 1½–2 pounds halibut, cut into individual portions
- ¼ cup heavy cream or coconut milk
- ½ lemon

1. Preheat the oven to 350°F.

2. Cut off and discard the bottom root parts and the green hard parts of the leeks (or save them for making stock). Slice the remaining parts of the leeks in half lengthwise, then widthwise into ¼-inch slices. Place in a colander or mesh strainer and rinse thoroughly to remove any dirt caught between the layers.

3. In a Dutch oven or deep oven-safe pan, melt the butter or ghee over medium heat, add the garlic and sliced leeks, season with salt and pepper, and stir to coat the leeks well. Sauté for 2–3 minutes or until they begin to soften.

4. Add the white wine, scrape any stuck bits from the bottom of the pan, stir in the thyme, and bring to a simmer. Cover and bake for 30–35 minutes or until the leeks are very tender.

5. Season the halibut with salt and pepper. Nestle the halibut in the leeks, pour the heavy cream or coconut milk over the halibut, cover, and bake for 15–20 more minutes or until the halibut flakes easily with a fork.

6. Remove the halibut from the pan, place it on a warmed tray, and tent with foil to keep warm. Put the pan back on the stovetop over medium heat, squeeze the lemon juice into the sauce, and reduce until slightly thick.

7. Serve the halibut with leeks and sauce spooned on top or on the side.

mediterranean halibut with
citrus vinaigrette and black olives

Quite often a sauce is used to flavor a light-tasting fish or meat, but making a sauce isn't always practical for a quick meal. And not everyone appreciates a plain old salt-and-peppered meal when you don't have the time to make a sauce. A vinaigrette is a great shortcut in this situation. Making a quick and easy vinaigrette gives this mild, soft-fleshed fish a smooth and vibrant finish with just a few extra steps.

- 2 tablespoons finely chopped fresh parsley
- 2 tablespoons finely chopped fresh cilantro
- 1 tablespoon minced fresh rosemary
- 3 cloves garlic, minced
- 1½ pounds halibut, cut into individual portions
- 1 tablespoon avocado oil
- salt and pepper to taste
- 2 tablespoons ghee
- ⅓ cup extra-virgin olive oil
- juice of 1 lemon
- juice of 1 lime
- 2 teaspoons brown mustard
- ½ cup black olives

1. In a small bowl, mix together the parsley, cilantro, rosemary, and garlic. Brush each halibut fillet with avocado oil and season with salt and pepper, then pat with the herb and garlic mixture.

2. In a large pan, heat the ghee over medium-high heat, then add the halibut, making sure not to overcrowd the pan. Cook for 2—3 minutes or until nicely browned, then flip, reduce the heat to medium, and cook for 4—5 more minutes or until the fish flakes easily with a fork.

3. In a small bowl, whisk together the olive oil, lemon juice, lime juice, and mustard for the citrus vinaigrette. Serve the halibut with the olives and a drizzle of the vinaigrette on top.

thai fish cakes

serves 5—6

This is my version of Thai fish cakes, also known as tod mun pla. I did my best to make them as traditional as possible, but with more fresh ingredients. People typically make Thai fish cakes with a premade fish or shrimp paste, which I personally don't like. Instead, I make my own fish paste with fresh halibut and shrimp. Not only is it incredibly fast and easy to prepare, but it's also packed with robust and vibrant Thai flavors. Your dinner companions will think that you stole the recipe from a Thai grandmother.

- 1 pound halibut
- ½ pound shrimp
- 1½ tablespoons red curry paste
- 2 teaspoons fish sauce
- 2 tablespoons chopped fresh cilantro
- 1 egg
- 1 kaffir lime leaf, sliced thin, or zest of 1 lime
- ⅓ cup green beans, stems trimmed, chopped into ¼-inch pieces
- 3 tablespoons ghee or lard
- lime wedges for serving

1. In a food processor, place the halibut, shrimp, red curry paste, fish sauce, cilantro, egg, and lime leaf or zest and process until you have a smooth paste.

2. Transfer the paste to a bowl and mix in the green beans. With wet hands, form the mixture into patties and refrigerate for 10 minutes.

3. In a large pan, heat the ghee or lard over medium-high heat. Fry the fish cakes in batches to avoid overcrowding the pan, 2—3 minutes per side or until each fish cake is cooked through. Serve immediately with the lime wedges on the side.

grilled mahi mahi with roasted tomatillo salsa

Just because you may not be using tortilla chips for dipping doesn't mean that salsa no longer has a place in your life. I like to use salsa as a sauce for meats or as a braising liquid. In this recipe, homemade tomatillo salsa is spooned on top of grilled mahi mahi.

- 1½ pounds mahi mahi fillets, cut into individual portions
- salt and pepper to taste
- 1 tablespoon ghee or avocado oil
- Roasted Tomatillo Salsa for serving (page 253)

1. Preheat a gas grill to high heat.

2. Season the mahi mahi fillets with salt and pepper. Just before placing them on the grill, brush the grates with the ghee or avocado oil, then place the fish on the greased grates. Reduce the heat to medium-high and grill for 3 minutes per side. Lower the heat to medium, close the lid, and grill for 2—3 more minutes or until the fish is opaque and flakes easily with a fork.

3. Serve the fish with Roasted Tomatillo Salsa on top.

pistachio-crusted salmon

With its light pink flesh studded with vibrant green pistachios, this salmon presents wonderfully. Even though it looks incredibly complex, it's easy enough for anyone to make. With just a little effort you get a gorgeously dressed salmon fillet that's perfect for company or a quick weeknight meal.

- 1 (1½–2 pounds) salmon fillet, skin on
- salt and pepper to taste
- ¼ cup Dijon mustard
- 1 tablespoon chopped fresh chives
- ½ cup shelled pistachios, crushed

1. Preheat the oven to 400°F and line a baking sheet with parchment paper.

2. Season the skin side of the salmon with salt and pepper. Place the salmon skin side down on the parchment-lined baking sheet. In a small bowl, mix the mustard with the chives, then coat the salmon fillet with the mustard mixture. Lightly press the crushed pistachios all over the salmon.

3. Bake for 15—20 minutes or until the fish flakes easily with a fork.

sea bass with fennel and tomato

Fatty fish like Chilean sea bass is a nice change of pace from the more common types such as halibut and cod, because its texture and flavor are significantly richer. I prefer sea bass paired with vibrant and refreshing ingredients like tomatoes and fennel, which help cut the richness of the fish and keep the meal from feeling too heavy. Letting the fish braise in the fruity white wine broth enrobes it in their flavors—and the fish gives off some of its fat to flavor the broth as well. Once the braise is done, you can almost serve this dish as a one-pot meal because the fish is so rich and there are just enough vegetables and broth to satisfy everyone.

- 2 tablespoons ghee
- 3 cloves garlic, thinly sliced
- 1 bulb fennel, cored and thinly sliced
- 2 shallots, thinly sliced
- 2 tomatoes, coarsely chopped
- ¼ cup chicken Mother Stock (page 144)
- ⅓ cup white wine
- salt and pepper to taste
- 1 lemon, sliced into thin rounds
- ⅓ cup kalamata olives
- 1½ pounds sea bass, cut into individual portions

1. Heat the ghee in a large pot or Dutch oven over medium heat. Add the garlic, fennel, and shallots and cook, stirring occasionally, for 3 minutes or until the shallots begin to soften. Stir in the tomatoes and cook for 1 additional minute, then pour in the chicken stock and white wine, scraping the bottom of the pot. Season with salt and pepper. Bring the broth to a simmer and add the lemon slices and kalamata olives.

2. Season the sea bass with salt and pepper, then nestle the fish pieces in the broth. Make sure that the broth is still simmering, then reduce the heat to low, cover, and cook for 15—20 minutes or until the fish is opaque and flakes easily with a fork.

3. Serve the fish on top of the vegetables with a generous amount of the broth.

coriander and mustard seed tuna steaks with ginger aioli

serves 4

Seared tuna steaks should be rare to medium-rare. When you cook them through too much, they lose a lot of their flavor. I like to coat my tuna steaks with a crunchy layer of spices that creates a fragrant crust around the fish. To introduce a little richness, I serve the crusted tuna with a slightly sweet and umami-packed ginger aioli made with fresh homemade mayonnaise.

- 3 tablespoons coriander seeds
- 1 tablespoon mustard seed
- ¼ teaspoon salt
- ½ teaspoon coarse-ground pepper
- 4 (6–7 ounce) ahi tuna steaks (1 inch thick)
- avocado oil for brushing
- 1½ tablespoons ghee

for the aioli:

- ⅓ cup Mayonnaise (page 252)
- ½ teaspoon fish sauce
- ½ tablespoon coconut aminos or tamari
- ½ teaspoon toasted sesame oil
- 2 teaspoons unseasoned rice vinegar
- 1 clove garlic, grated
- 1-inch knob of ginger, peeled and grated

1. In a food processor, add the coriander seeds, mustard seed, salt, and pepper and pulse until you get a coarse powder. Brush the tuna fillets with avocado oil on both sides, then pat each fillet with the spice mixture.

2. Heat the ghee in a large pan over medium-high heat until very hot, then add the tuna, spacing the fillets evenly to keep them from overcrowding the pan. Sear for 3 minutes per side, then immediately remove from the heat.

3. In a small bowl, combine the Mayonnaise, fish sauce, coconut aminos or tamari, toasted sesame oil, rice vinegar, garlic, and ginger and whisk until well incorporated. Serve the fish with the aioli on top or on the side.

shrimp scampi

My mom used to be the worst about eating seafood. She wouldn't go within 10 feet of freshly cooked salmon. If she went to a seafood restaurant, she almost always ordered the shrimp scampi because of her fear of fish. I think I've done a pretty good job of reforming her; now she eats practically every fish in the sea, with the exception of squid. Nonetheless, she still loves the garlic-enriched and citrusy flavor of shrimp scampi, so I made a version of her favorite. This is one of the easiest recipes to tackle in this book, yet it tastes like you spent hours slaving over the stove perfecting its fresh and powerful flavor.

- 2 tablespoons butter or ghee
- 5 cloves garlic, minced
- ½ teaspoon red pepper flakes
- 1½ pounds shrimp, peeled and deveined
- ⅓ cup white wine
- juice of 1 lemon
- 3 tablespoons chopped fresh parsley
- extra-virgin olive oil for drizzling

1. Heat the butter or ghee in a large pan over medium heat. Add the garlic and red pepper flakes and cook until fragrant, then add the shrimp and toss to coat. Cook for 5—8 minutes or until the shrimp is opaque and cooked through. Add the white wine and reduce by half, then add the lemon juice and parsley and toss once more.

2. Serve with a drizzle of olive oil, about 2 teaspoons per person.

grilled king crab legs with coconut-tomato sauce

When I eat crab, I typically have it with a dose of butter or ghee on the side for dipping. In this recipe, I decided to step outside of my usual habits and try something a little more extravagant and fun. The slightly sweet and creamy coconut-tomato sauce complements the lightness of the crab in a way that may be even better than butter. Okay, maybe not—nothing trumps butter—but I would call this a close runner-up.

for the sauce:

- 1 tablespoon coconut oil
- 1 clove garlic, thinly sliced
- 1 shallot, thinly sliced
- ¼ teaspoon fennel seeds
- ¼ cup peeled and diced tomatoes
- ½ cup coconut milk
- ¼ teaspoon cayenne pepper
- 2 teaspoons fish sauce

- 2½ pounds king crab legs
- lime wedges for serving

1. Heat the coconut oil in a medium-sized saucepan over medium heat. Add the garlic, shallot, and fennel seeds and sauté for 3—4 minutes or until the shallot is soft. Add the tomatoes, coconut milk, cayenne pepper, and fish sauce and leave to simmer, covered.

2. While the sauce is simmering, grill the king crab legs on high heat for 8—10 minutes, flipping occasionally, until the shells are lightly browned and the crab meat is hot.

3. Remove the sauce from the heat. Serve the crab legs with lime wedges and sauce on the side.

broiled lobster tails with garlic-parsley butter

Cooking lobster is daunting to many people because they think that they have to handle live lobsters. But at a local grocery store, you can actually buy the tails separately—a much better option for someone who wants to cook lobster but isn't quite ready to cook a live one. Butterflied lobster tails broiled with a garlicky parsley butter work for any occasion. They are fast and easy to make, yet look and taste incredibly elegant.

- 4 tablespoons butter or ghee, melted
- 5 cloves garlic, minced
- 2 tablespoons minced fresh parsley, plus more for garnish
- 4 large or 8 small lobster tails
- salt and pepper to taste

1. Line a baking sheet with aluminum foil.

2. In a small bowl, combine the butter or ghee, garlic, and parsley. Cut the lobster tails along the top all the way down the shell. Flip the tails over and cut along the bottom all the way down the shell. Flip the tails over again so that the top of the shell is facing you, and open them like a book to expose the flesh. Place them on the foil-lined baking sheet.

3. Coat the lobster tails with the garlic-parsley butter and reserve any left over for serving. Season with salt and pepper and broil on high for 6–7 minutes or until completely opaque. Serve with a sprinkle of parsley.

seared scallops with saffron-morel sauce

Of the many shellfish that exist in the sea, scallops are by far my favorite. When seared properly, they're tender and slightly sweet. Seared scallops on their own are quite nice, but they are even more of an experience when served with a creamy and piquant sauce like this one.

- ½ ounce dried morel mushrooms
- 1 cup hot water
- 1½ tablespoons ghee
- 1 pound jumbo sea scallops
- salt and pepper to taste
- 2 tablespoons butter
- 1 shallot, minced
- 2 cloves garlic, minced
- 6 saffron threads, crushed
- ½ tablespoon red wine vinegar
- ¼ cup heavy cream or coconut milk

1. Place the dried morels in a small bowl, pour the hot water over them, and let soak for 25 minutes. Once the morels have soaked, reserve the soaking liquid, ring out the morels to remove the excess moisture, and place them in a separate bowl.

2. Heat the ghee in a large pan over medium-high heat until very hot. Pat the scallops dry and season them with salt and pepper, then sear them for 1–2 minutes per side. Remove the seared scallops from the pan, reduce the heat to medium, and add the butter. Once the butter begins to bubble, add the shallot, garlic, and saffron. Cook, stirring, for 3–4 minutes or until the shallot is softened.

3. Pour in the mushroom soaking liquid while scraping the bottom of the pan with a wooden spoon, and reduce the sauce by half. Stir in the vinegar and heavy cream or coconut milk, season with salt and pepper, and add the mushrooms. Bring to a simmer and reduce until the sauce thickens slightly, about 1 minute.

4. Serve the scallops with the sauce and mushrooms.

avocado-lime scallop ceviche

When the heat of summer sets in, my parents and I like to take a trip to paradise. One of the moments I look forward to most is eating a bowl of freshly made, ice-cold ceviche while digging my toes in the warm sand. Ceviche is made by "cooking" fish in an acid such as lemon or lime juice. I created this recipe to tide us over until our next trip.

- 1 pound jumbo sea scallops
- ½ cup plus 1 tablespoon fresh-squeezed lime juice
- salt to taste
- ⅓ cup minced fresh cilantro
- ½ cup diced red onion

1. Cut the scallops into ½-inch chunks. Place in a container, pour in the lime juice, and season with salt. Cover and refrigerate for at least 3 hours and up to 16 hours.

2. Stir in the cilantro and red onion and serve immediately.

Note: Make sure to get your juice from fresh limes; otherwise, the result could end up tasting bitter.

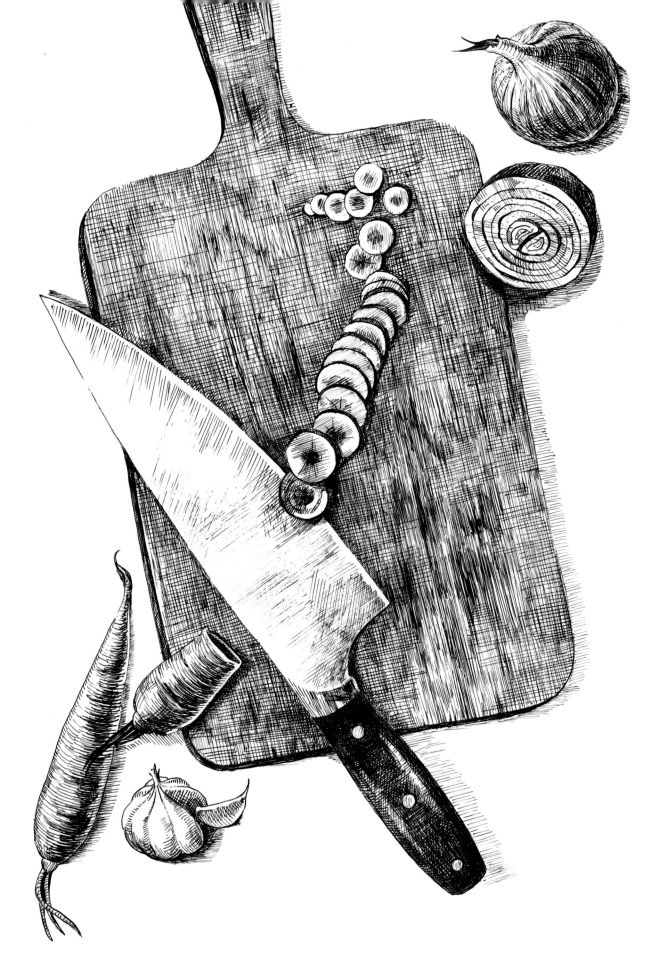

soups and stews

mother stock

In any kitchen, it's incredibly important to have stock on hand for use in soups, braises, sauces, and much more. I always have stock in my fridge or freezer because I utilize both fresh bones and bones that I have trimmed off of something prior to cooking it. For example, I like to save chicken bones when I cook a whole chicken by simply removing the bones before eating and placing them in a designated freezer bag. If you do so religiously, you will always have bones for making stock.

- 3 pounds animal bones and pieces (beef, chicken, lamb, or pork)
- 1 large onion, coarsely chopped
- 2 medium carrots, coarsely chopped
- 1 large stalk celery, coarsely chopped
- 2 bay leaves
- salt and pepper to taste

Notes: By "animal bones and pieces," I mean mainly bones with the addition of some meaty pieces if you like. You want a high ratio of bones to meaty pieces. Meatier bones make for an even better stock.

You can also make this stock overnight in a slow cooker, following the same method of pouring in enough water to cover the bones and other ingredients.

to make in a pressure cooker:

1. Place the animal bones and pieces, onion, carrots, celery, and bay leaves in a pressure cooker. Add just enough water to cover the vegetables and bones so that everything is submerged, making sure not to fill the pressure cooker more than two-thirds of the way.

2. Season generously with salt and pepper, then lock the lid. Bring it to high pressure over high heat. Once it reaches high pressure, immediately reduce the heat to low, and cook at high pressure for at least 45 minutes, but preferably 1 hour. Remove from the heat and let the pressure release naturally.

3. Strain the stock through a mesh sieve into a heat-proof bowl, pressing the solids against the sieve to extract as much flavor as possible.

to make in a stockpot:

1. In a large pot, add the animal bones and pieces and just enough water to cover. Bring to a boil and season generously with salt and pepper, then reduce the heat and simmer for 5—6 hours, skimming the top occasionally. Add a little bit of water if the bones begin to stick out of the water.

2. Add the onion, carrots, celery, and bay leaves and simmer for another hour, then strain through a mesh sieve into a heat-proof bowl, pressing the solids against the sieve to extract as much flavor as possible.

You can skim off the fat immediately, but it's much easier to refrigerate the stock first to allow the fat to harden at the top and then scrape it off. Store the stock in the fridge for up to 1 week or in the freezer for as long as you like.

broccoli soup

To me, this recipe exemplifies the beauty of simplicity when cooking with fresh vegetables from the farmers' market. It's really as simple as broccoli, water, and some salt and pepper. The flavor of broccoli itself is actually quite gorgeous, but sometimes I like to add an extra touch of richness with a little bit of tart and creamy goat cheese and crunchy walnuts.

- 3 stalks broccoli
- 5½ cups water
- salt and pepper to taste
- add-ins: crumbled goat cheese and crushed walnuts (optional)
- extra-virgin olive oil for drizzling

1. Trim off the broccoli stems so that you're left with only the florets. Bring $5\frac{1}{2}$ cups water to a boil in a medium-sized pot over high heat. Add the broccoli and season with salt and pepper. Cover, lower the heat to medium-high, and boil for 5 — 7 minutes or until the broccoli is easily pierced with a fork.

2. Strain the liquid into a medium-sized bowl. Place the broccoli in a blender and pour in the strained liquid just to the top of the broccoli. Add salt and pepper and blend until completely smooth.

3. Serve with goat cheese and crushed walnuts (if using) crumbled in the bottom of each bowl and a drizzle of olive oil on top.

chilled coconut, avocado, and cucumber soup

Avocados are one of my favorite things to have with a meal because they are so filling and add a wonderful textural sensation when eaten with another bite of food. This cold soup combines avocados with creamy coconut milk to make a light, silky dish that is wonderfully refreshing when served on a hot day.

- ½ cup unsweetened coconut flakes
- 2 medium ripe avocados, pitted
- 1 medium cucumber
- 1 cup coconut milk
- 1 bunch fresh basil (7–8 large leaves)
- ¼ teaspoon chipotle chili powder
- salt and pepper to taste

1. Preheat the oven to 325°F and line a baking sheet with parchment paper.

2. Spread the coconut flakes on the parchment-lined baking sheet and bake for 4–5 minutes or until they begin to turn golden brown around the edges.

3. Place the remaining ingredients in a blender and purée until completely smooth. Chill in the refrigerator for 20 minutes before serving.

tom kha gai with chili oil

Thai food never ceases to amaze me with its sensationally unique uses of flavor. There is nothing like the flavor of a classic Thai dish like tom kha gai. I like to soak dried shiitake mushrooms and use the soaking liquid as a mushroom stock to enhance the soup with a rich umami flavor profile. Along with the mushroom stock, fragrant roots, herbs, and spices meld in this slightly sweet and milky soup flecked with vibrant orange dots of tongue-tingling chili oil.

- 1 ounce dried shiitake mushrooms
- 2 cups hot water
- ¼ cup macadamia nut oil
- 1½ tablespoons red chili flakes
- 1 cup chicken Mother Stock (page 144)
- 2 stalks lemongrass, cut into 1-inch pieces and smashed
- 4 kaffir lime leaves or 2 teaspoons lime zest
- 4½-inch knob of ginger, peeled and thinly sliced
- 1½ pounds boneless, skinless chicken thighs or breasts, cut into bite-sized pieces
- 1 (13.5-ounce) can coconut milk
- 2 tablespoons fish sauce
- 2 limes, cut into wedges
- ½ cup chopped fresh cilantro

1. Place the dried shiitake mushrooms in a bowl, pour the hot water over them, cover with foil, and let sit for 20 minutes.

2. In a small skillet over medium heat, warm the macadamia nut oil, then add the chili flakes and swish them around for a minute or two. The chili flakes should foam when they go in. Pour the hot oil into a heat-safe container and let sit for 15 minutes, then strain through a mesh sieve into a separate container and discard the chili flakes.

3. Once the mushrooms have soaked for 20 minutes, wring them out over the bowl in which you soaked them. Pour the soaking liquid into a medium-sized pot along with the chicken stock, lemongrass, lime leaves or zest, and ginger. Bring to a boil, then reduce the heat and simmer, uncovered, for 12 minutes. Strain the broth through a mesh sieve over a heat-proof container, then pour the steeped broth back into the pot.

4. Bring the broth to a boil. Add the chicken and soaked mushrooms, then reduce the heat and simmer for 20 minutes or until the chicken is cooked through. Stir in the coconut milk and fish sauce.

5. Serve the soup with lime wedges, cilantro, and chili oil on top.

Note: The chili oil is very spicy and should be added drop by drop depending on your heat preference.

asparagus soup with crispy shallots

serves 3—4

During a small adventure in New York with my brother, I was served a couple of dishes with a side of crispy shallots that I could use to garnish to my heart's desire. After discovering the beauty of crispy shallots, I knew that they would be good on absolutely anything. My first test when I got back home was this soup topped with said crispy shallots, and it was perfection. The fresh, vibrant soup pairs tremendously well with the nutty-tasting and crunchy shallots.

for the crispy shallots:

- 3 tablespoons lard
- 2 shallots, thinly sliced
- salt and pepper to taste

for the soup:

- 2 pounds asparagus, trimmed
- 2 tablespoons butter or ghee
- 1 shallot, minced
- 3 sage leaves, minced
- salt and pepper to taste
- 4 cups chicken Mother Stock (page 144)
- ½ cup water

1. Heat the lard in a medium-sized pan over low heat. Add the sliced shallots and cook, stirring often, for 10—12 minutes or until they turn a dark golden brown. Place the crispy shallots on a paper towel and season with salt and pepper.

2. Cut off and reserve the tips of the asparagus. Chop the stalks into thin rounds about ¼-inch thick. Heat the butter or ghee in a medium-sized pot, add the asparagus rounds and minced shallot, and sauté for about 5 minutes. Stir in the sage and season with salt and pepper. Pour in the chicken stock, bring to a boil, then reduce the heat to low and simmer, uncovered, for 10—15 minutes or until the asparagus is tender.

3. While the soup is simmering, bring the water to a boil in a separate pot. Add the asparagus tips and boil for 3 minutes. Drain, place in an ice water bath for 2 minutes, and then remove from the ice bath.

4. Once the soup is done simmering, purée it in batches in a blender until completely smooth. Take care when puréeing the soup, as it will be very hot. Taste for seasoning and add salt and pepper as desired. Serve with the crispy shallots and asparagus tips on top.

egg drop soup

One of my hands-down favorite soups is egg drop soup. The thought of that warm and fragrant broth paired with silky strands of egg makes me want a big, steaming bowl in front of me. When I was young, my friend Chase and I would always order a large serving of egg drop soup from a local Chinese restaurant and happily gorge ourselves. Of course, that was before I changed my views on eating. Once I stopped eating out, I had the urge to make this soup myself. To my surprise, it was ridiculously easy and wonderfully satisfying.

- 4 cups chicken Mother Stock (page 144)
- 1 cinnamon stick
- ½-inch knob of ginger, peeled and thinly sliced
- 4 teaspoons fish sauce
- 1 teaspoon coconut aminos or tamari
- 1 tablespoon arrowroot starch
- 3 eggs, lightly beaten
- 3 green onions, sliced

1. Pour the chicken stock into a medium-sized saucepan over medium-high heat. When it begins to boil, lower the heat to medium-low. Add the cinnamon stick, ginger, fish sauce, and coconut aminos or tamari and simmer for 10 minutes.

2. Remove and discard the cinnamon stick and ginger. Place the arrowroot starch in a small bowl, pour in about ¼ cup of the broth, and whisk until completely dissolved without lumps. Slowly pour the arrowroot slurry into the broth, stirring until completely incorporated. Simmer for another minute, stirring often. If the arrowroot clumps, simply strain the broth through a mesh sieve into a bowl, pour the strained liquid back into the pot, and continue.

3. Holding the tines of a fork against the side of the bowl in which you beat the eggs, slowly pour the egg mixture into the hot broth, stirring constantly. Cook for about 1 minute to ensure that the eggs are cooked. Serve immediately, garnished with the sliced green onions.

roasted garlic soup

Any recipe that calls for 4 heads of garlic is okay in my book. We cook with a lot of garlic at my house because it's easy, fast, and flavorful. If you're worried about the flavor of this dish being too garlicky, trust me when I say that it isn't. Most of the garlic is slowly roasted until it's very light-tasting yet incredibly creamy, and perfect for puréeing into this rich and aromatic soup. Because garlic has powerful antimicrobial, antibiotic, and decongestant properties, I'm fairly sure that this soup would cure any ailment.

- 4 heads garlic, divided
- salt and pepper to taste
- 2 tablespoons avocado oil
- 2 tablespoons butter
- 2 medium leeks
- 3½ cups chicken Mother Stock (page 144)
- 1 teaspoon minced fresh thyme
- extra-virgin olive oil for drizzling

1. Preheat the oven to 400°F.

2. Remove the cloves from 3 of the heads of garlic, leaving them unpeeled. Place them in a small glass baking dish, season with salt and pepper, then drizzle the avocado oil over them and toss to coat. Cover the baking dish tightly with foil and roast for 30 minutes. Remove from the oven and let cool enough to handle without burning yourself.

3. Cut off and discard the bottom root parts and the green hard parts of the leeks. Slice the remaining parts of the leeks in half lengthwise and then into slices about 1/3-inch thick. Place the sliced leeks in a medium-sized bowl, fill with water, and swish the water around to rinse off any dirt. Drain the water.

4. Heat the butter in a medium-sized saucepan over medium heat. Add the leeks and sauté for 5—6 minutes or until soft. Peel the remaining head of garlic, add the raw peeled cloves to the leeks, then squeeze the roasted garlic cloves into the pan. Cook, stirring, for another 3 minutes, then add the chicken stock and increase the heat to medium-high until it begins to simmer. Reduce the heat to low and simmer, covered, for 20 minutes.

5. Purée the soup in batches in a blender with the thyme, seasoning with salt and pepper as needed. Take care when puréeing the soup, as it will be very hot. Serve with a drizzle of olive oil on top.

spiced butternut squash soup

During the colder months, butternut squash shows up all over the farmers' market. My mother and I adore butternut squash, so whenever there is a plethora, we tend to buy more than we know what to do with. The fastest way to get rid of an abundance of butternut squash is to make a soup out of it. I like to use classic, warm winter spices like cinnamon and nutmeg. I added those seasonings to this soup along with some of my other favorites spices to give it a slight edge.

for the spice mix:

- ¼ teaspoon coriander seeds
- ¼ teaspoon ancho chile powder
- small pinch of nutmeg
- ½ teaspoon cinnamon
- ¼ teaspoon pepper
- ½ teaspoon salt

for the soup:

- 2 tablespoons butter
- 1 small shallot, minced
- 3 cloves garlic, minced
- 1½-inch knob of ginger, peeled and thinly sliced
- 2½ pounds butternut squash, peeled and cut into 1-inch cubes
- 4 cups water
- salt and pepper to taste
- chopped walnuts for garnish (optional)

1. In a small pan over medium heat, toast the coriander seeds for 4 minutes, shaking the pan often to prevent burning. With a mortar and pestle or spice grinder, grind the coriander seeds until you have a fine powder.

2. In a small bowl, combine the ground coriander with the rest of the spice mix ingredients.

3. In a heavy pot over medium heat, heat the butter until it begins to bubble. Add the shallot, garlic, and ginger and cook until the shallot begins to soften, about 3 minutes. Add the cubed butternut squash and sauté for 4 minutes, then stir in the spice mix and cook for about 1 minute, stirring often to prevent burning. Pour in the water while scraping the bottom of the pot. Bring to a boil, then reduce the heat and simmer for 20 minutes or until squash is tender.

4. Carefully pour everything into a blender and purée until completely smooth. Season with salt and pepper and garnish with walnuts, if desired.

salmon soup

One day the refrigerator was pretty bare, but I really wanted to make a nice hearty soup for lunch. I gathered up whatever vegetables and meats I could find in a heap in front of me: salmon that was supposed to be for dinner, a bell pepper, and the rest of the ingredients you see in the list below. I tossed it all into a pot and simmered it, and the result was actually quite delicious. Now it's a recipe that I make quite often when I'm in a rush because it's so quick to prepare.

- 3 medium leeks

- 2 tablespoons butter or ghee

- 2 cloves garlic, minced

- 1 orange bell pepper, seeded, stemmed, de-ribbed, and sliced into strips

- 5 cups chicken Mother Stock (page 144)

- 2 teaspoons chopped fresh oregano

- salt and pepper to taste

- 1½ pounds salmon, skinned and cut into 2-inch cubes

- 3 tablespoons lemon juice

- 2 cups baby spinach

- lemon wedges for serving

1. Cut off and discard the bottom root parts and the green hard parts of the leeks (or save them for making stock). Slice the remaining parts of the leeks in half lengthwise and then into slices about ⅓-inch thick. Place the sliced leeks in a medium-sized bowl, fill with water, and swish the water around to rinse off any dirt. Drain the water and pat the leeks dry with a paper towel.

2. In a heavy-bottomed pot, heat the butter or ghee over medium heat. Add the leeks, garlic, and bell pepper and sauté for 4–5 minutes or until the leeks are very soft. Pour in the chicken stock while scraping the bottom of the pot with a wooden spoon, then add the oregano and season with salt and pepper.

3. Season the salmon with some additional salt and pepper. Bring the chicken stock to a boil, then add the salmon. Lower the heat immediately to medium-low and simmer for 5–7 minutes or until the salmon flakes easily with a fork.

4. Stir in the lemon juice and spinach and simmer for 3 more minutes or until the spinach wilts.

5. Serve the soup with lemon wedges on the side.

creamy veal stew

French cooking is a regional cuisine that I have always adored and respected. One of my favorite French dishes is a white veal stew known as *blanquette de veau,* which consists of veal shoulder braised and finished with cream. After learning about this dish, I attempted to make my own version. The result was this creamy yet light stew that is splendid any time of the year, regardless of the season. Veal shoulder is simmered and rendered utterly tender in white wine and beef broth, then finished with a stir of cream and pieces of vibrant asparagus to add a light touch to cut the richness.

- 3½ tablespoons ghee, divided
- 2½–3 pounds boneless veal shoulder, cut into 2-inch cubes
- salt and pepper to taste
- 4 large shallots, thinly sliced
- 2 carrots, diced
- ½ cup white wine
- 3 cups beef Mother Stock (page 144)
- 3 sprigs thyme
- 1 bay leaf
- 1 pound asparagus, trimmed and cut into 1½-inch pieces
- ¾ cup heavy cream or coconut milk
- 3½ tablespoons arrowroot starch
- ¼ cup water

1. In a large Dutch oven or pot over medium-high heat, heat 2½ tablespoons of the ghee. When the ghee is hot, season the veal with salt and pepper and brown it in batches to avoid overcrowding the pot. Place the browned pieces on a tray tented with foil.

2. Once all the veal is browned, dab the bottom of the pot with a paper towel, add the remaining 1 tablespoon ghee, and reduce the heat to medium. Add the shallots and carrots and sauté for 3 minutes or until the shallots begin to soften. Pour in the white wine and beef stock, scraping the bottom of the pot, then return the veal to the pot, add the thyme and bay leaf, and bring to a simmer. Season with salt and pepper, reduce the heat to low, and cover, then quickly remove from the heat. Place a diffuser on the burner, place the pot on the diffused burner, and simmer for 2 hours.

3. Add the asparagus, cover, and cook for 15—20 minutes or until the asparagus is tender. Stir in the heavy cream or coconut milk. In a small bowl, mix the arrowroot starch with the water, then pour in a little bit of the hot stew. Slowly pour the arrowroot mixture into the pot, stirring slowly, until it thickens, about 30 seconds.

texas chili

My mother and her side of the family are all native-born Texans, so to them, chili is a precise and sacred art. We prefer a meaty and thick-sauced chili that is just slightly warm and not too spicy. I made my chili with all these traits in mind, and with the hope of competing with my uncles. My Uncle Larry gave it his approval, so I feel pretty accomplished, because that man knows his chili. There is no specification for what makes it a Texas chili other than that it was made by an "honorary Texan"—a title given to me by my Texas relatives. While I'm aware that the list of ingredients is daunting, I promise it isn't as bad as you might think; many of these ingredients are likely in your kitchen already, and if they're not, they should be fairly easy to find.

- 3 dried ancho chiles
- 1 dried guajillo chile
- 2 cups hot water
- 1 red bell pepper
- ¾ teaspoon chipotle chili powder
- 1 tablespoon unsweetened cacao powder
- 1 teaspoon coriander
- ½ teaspoon cinnamon
- 2 teaspoons ground cumin
- 2 pounds boneless beef chuck roast, cut into 1-inch chunks
- 1 pound boneless short ribs, cut into 1-inch chunks
- salt and pepper to taste
- 3½ tablespoons lard or avocado oil, divided
- 1 large onion, chopped
- 3 cloves garlic, minced
- 5 tablespoons apple cider vinegar
- 2 cups beef Mother Stock (page 144)
- 1¼ cups crushed tomatoes
- 3 sprigs marjoram
- 1 bay leaf
- ¼ cup cold water
- 3 tablespoons arrowroot starch

1. Snip the ends off the dried chiles and shake out the seeds. In a small skillet over medium heat, toast the chiles for 2—3 minutes or until fragrant and slightly softened. Place the toasted chiles in a medium-sized bowl, cover with the hot water, and soak for 20 minutes or until very soft.

2. While the chiles are soaking, place the bell pepper on a burner over medium heat, directly over the flame, and char on all sides, then place in a bowl covered with foil. Once the chiles have soaked, remove the charred skin from the bell pepper and remove the seeds and stem.

3. Place the soaked chiles and soaking liquid in a blender along with the charred bell pepper, chipotle chili powder, cacao powder, coriander, cinnamon, and cumin and purée until smooth.

4. Season the meat with salt and pepper. In a large pot or Dutch oven, heat 2½ tablespoons of the lard or avocado oil over medium-high heat. Brown the meat in batches, 2—3 minutes per side, until well browned, placing the browned pieces on a tray tented with foil. Once all the meat is browned, reduce the heat to medium and heat the remaining 1 tablespoon lard or avocado oil. Add the onion and garlic and sauté for 3—4 minutes or until softened.

5. Add the pureed chile mixture, vinegar, stock, and crushed tomatoes, scraping the bottom of the pot to remove any stuck bits. Season with salt and pepper and bring to a light simmer, then add the browned meat along with the marjoram and bay leaf. Reduce the heat to low, cover, and simmer for 3½—4 hours or until the meat is fork-tender. Around a third of the way through cooking, check to see if it's simmering too hard; if it is, place a diffuser over the burner and continue cooking.

6. In a small bowl, make a slurry by whisking the cold water and arrowroot starch thoroughly. Whisk about 1 tablespoon of the hot chili into the slurry, then slowly pour the slurry into the chili, stirring gently until the chili thickens.

——— vegetables ———

vinaigrette-marinated
squash noodles

serves 4

Vegetable noodles are an interesting and unique way to serve squash. Giving these squash noodles some time to marinate in a tart and awakening vinaigrette saturates them with its flavor. Each bite sings of the vinaigrette, while the noodles are much lighter and tamer than they are when they are raw.

for the vinaigrette marinade:

- ¼ cup extra-virgin olive oil
- ¼ cup white wine vinegar
- ½ shallot, minced
- 1 teaspoon Dijon mustard
- generous pinch of salt

for the noodles:

- 1 yellow squash
- 1 zucchini
- 1 tablespoon capers
- pepper to taste

1. In a small bowl, whisk all the vinaigrette marinade ingredients until well combined.

2. With a vegetable spiral slicer or the julienne setting on a mandoline, make noodles out of the yellow squash and zucchini.

3. In a large bowl, add the zucchini noodles, yellow squash noodles, and capers, then pour the vinaigrette marinade over them and stir until thoroughly coated.

4. Refrigerate for at least 2 hours or up to 24 hours.

5. Before serving, mix some fresh-ground pepper into the noodles.

roasted asparagus with toasted hazelnuts and lemon

serves 4

During the spring and summer, I can't get enough of asparagus. Stores are stocked with organic bunches (even though it's not necessary to buy organic asparagus), and my local farms begin producing it like mad. I always used to cook asparagus in a pan with some cooking fat over fairly high heat so that I could get crispy edges on it. That all changed when I started roasting asparagus. The beautiful, tightly wrapped tips become irresistibly crispy, and the entire stalk acquires a smoky and slightly sweet taste.

- 2 pounds asparagus, trimmed
- salt and pepper to taste
- 2 tablespoons avocado oil or melted ghee
- 1 lemon, cut into ½-inch slices
- ⅓ cup hazelnuts
- 3 tablespoons chopped fresh parsley

1. Preheat the oven to 400°F and line a baking sheet with aluminum foil.

2. Season the asparagus with salt and pepper and toss in the avocado oil or melted ghee. Place on the baking sheet spaced evenly apart, top with the lemon slices, and roast for 8–10 minutes or until tender, then broil for 4 minutes until the tips are browned and slightly crispy.

3. While the asparagus is roasting, toast the hazelnuts in a small pan over medium heat for about 4 minutes or until they begin to brown and become fragrant. Coarsely chop the hazelnuts.

4. Serve the roasted asparagus sprinkled with the chopped hazelnuts and parsley.

fragrant indian
cauliflower "couscous"

serves 4

In New York City, I discovered an Indian restaurant that serves a fragrant rice with its roasted lamb dishes. The rice tastes exactly like its name implies: incredibly spiced and powerfully flavored, making it a perfect accompaniment to liven up a meat dish. This "couscous" exhibits the same traits, but in a more nutrient-packed and healthful way.

for the spice mix:

- ¾ teaspoon ground cumin
- ½ teaspoon paprika
- ¼ teaspoon mustard powder
- ¼ teaspoon ground ginger
- ¼ teaspoon pepper
- ¼ teaspoon cinnamon
- pinch of ground cloves

- 1 head cauliflower, trimmed
- 2 tablespoons coconut oil
- 3 shallots, minced
- 4 cloves garlic, minced
- juice of 1 lime
- 1 tablespoon fish sauce
- 3 cardamom pods
- 1 cinnamon stick
- ¼ cup chopped fresh cilantro

1. Combine all the spice mix ingredients in a small bowl.

2. Cut the cauliflower into small, uniform pieces and pulse in batches in a food processor until you get a couscous-like consistency.

3. In a large pan, heat the coconut oil, then add the shallots and garlic and cook until the shallots are softened, 3–4 minutes. Add the spice mix, stirring often to prevent burning, and cook for 1 minute, then stir in the cauliflower, lime juice, and fish sauce. Add the cardamom pods and cinnamon stick and reduce the heat to low. Cover and cook for 10 minutes.

4. Serve the cauliflower couscous garnished with chopped cilantro.

five-spice eggplant rounds

My mom has always been smart when it comes to making dinner in a hurry. Typically it's cooked in a pan or broiled to speed things up. Broiling eggplant imparts a smoky sweetness, making it a perfect candidate for spicing. You can spice it with practically any dry spice and mix and match your flavors to create a plethora of unique outcomes. I prefer to flavor my eggplant with a subtle hit of garlic and a fragrant addition of Chinese five-spice.

- 2 medium eggplants
- 4 cloves garlic, left in skins
- 2 tablespoons melted ghee or avocado oil
- 2 teaspoons Chinese five-spice powder
- salt and pepper to taste

1. Slice the eggplants about ½-inch thick, then slice each garlic clove in half, leaving them in their skins.

2. Line a baking sheet with aluminum foil, spread the eggplant rounds in an even layer on the baking sheet, and scatter the sliced garlic cloves around the eggplant. Drizzle the melted ghee or avocado oil all over, then sprinkle with Chinese five-spice powder and salt and pepper.

3. Broil for 6—7 minutes, then flip the eggplant rounds and broil for an additional 3—4 minutes or until nicely browned on the outside and tender in the middle.

caramelized butternut squash
with thyme

I have a minor obsession with getting proper caramelization on just about everything. Caramelization makes a dish at least twice as good because it adds just the right amount of sweetness, as well as a sticky, silky texture. If you can get butternut squash properly caramelized, you won't turn back.

- 1–1½ pounds butternut squash, peeled and cut into 1-inch cubes
- 2½ tablespoons melted ghee or avocado oil
- salt and pepper to taste
- 1 tablespoon chopped fresh thyme

1. Preheat the oven to 400°F. Line a baking sheet with aluminum foil.

2. Toss the butternut squash with the melted ghee or avocado oil, salt and pepper, and thyme.

3. Pour the butternut squash onto the lined baking sheet and roast for 40—45 minutes. If it's not crispy and caramelized enough for you, broil it for 3—4 minutes or until the desired crispiness is achieved.

grilled eggplant and tomato stacks

serves 4

My friend Izy, who runs the food blog Top with Cinnamon, introduced me to grilled eggplant. Well, I knew that it existed, but Izy is the one who insisted that I try it. Grilling eggplant imparts a wonderfully deep, smoky flavor. Here, it pairs beautifully with fresh tomatoes and sweet balsamic vinegar, all stacked up in a beautiful tower.

- 1 large globe eggplant, cut into ½-inch slices
- 2 tablespoons avocado oil
- salt and pepper to taste
- 2 large tomatoes, cut into ½-inch slices
- 4 ounces goat brie, sliced (optional)
- 2 tablespoons extra-virgin olive oil
- 2 tablespoons balsamic vinegar
- 2 teaspoons chopped fresh thyme

1. Preheat a gas grill to medium-high heat. Brush both sides of the eggplant slices with the avocado oil and season with salt and pepper. Grill until soft, about 3−4 minutes per side.

2. Assemble 2 stacks by topping a slice of eggplant with a slice of tomato, then another eggplant slice, a goat brie slice (if using), a tomato slice, an eggplant slice, a goat brie slice, a tomato slice, and an eggplant slice.

3. Drizzle the stacks with olive oil and balsamic vinegar, season with salt and pepper, and garnish with thyme.

asparagus and sugar snap pea salad with spring onions

Something about the crunch of an ice-cold salad makes it exciting. Sugar snap peas are an excellent addition to a salad, as long as you steam them just enough that they retain their vibrant crunch and don't become paste-like. I've kept this salad simple to focus on the natural, fresh taste of the vegetables, which are only subtly spiked by refreshing lemon, extra-virgin olive oil, and spring onions.

- 2 pounds asparagus, trimmed
- 6 ounces sugar snap peas, trimmed
- 1 lemon, zested and juiced
- ⅓ cup extra-virgin olive oil
- 2 spring onions or green onions, sliced
- salt and pepper to taste

1. In a steamer basket over boiling water, steam the asparagus and sugar snap peas for 4—5 minutes or until tender. Plunge the steamed vegetables in an ice water bath until cold, then drain.

2. In a medium-sized bowl, combine the asparagus, sugar snap peas, lemon zest and juice, olive oil, onions, and salt and pepper.

3. Serve immediately on chilled plates.

balsamic-glazed onions
and grape tomatoes

I developed this recipe at my brother Nick's apartment. I was grilling some grass-fed dry-aged steaks with Nick and his wife, Julia, and I had to whip up something to serve with them. We had picked up some fresh grape tomatoes at the farmers' market earlier that morning, so one thing led to another, and this dish came to be. Sweet onions and grape tomatoes are caramelized in a sticky reduced balsamic sauce, making a perfect topper for a steak or a side by itself.

- 2 tablespoons butter or ghee
- 1 medium onion, thinly sliced
- 3 cloves garlic, thinly sliced
- 1 pint grape tomatoes
- salt to taste
- 1½ tablespoons balsamic vinegar

1. In a medium saucepan, heat the butter or ghee over medium heat until hot. Add the onion and garlic, reduce the heat to medium-low, and sauté for 5 minutes or until softened.

2. Add the grape tomatoes, season generously with salt, increase the heat to medium, and sauté for 8 minutes. Increase the heat to medium-high and stir in the balsamic vinegar. Let bubble for 2−3 minutes, stirring constantly, until the vinegar has thickened and coats the onions thoroughly.

thai salad

When I lived in California, there was a Thai restaurant that we always went to after a movie. My mom would order their refreshing and crunchy salad, which had a coating of semi-sweet, creamy peanut dressing. I wasn't much of a salad eater then, so I typically just tasted the dressing. Luckily, I enjoy vegetables now and have done my best to re-create the dish according to my own eating principles.

- 2 large carrots
- 5 radishes
- 1 medium head cabbage
- 1 cup chopped fresh cilantro

- 1 recipe Ginger-Almond Dressing (page 248)

1. With a vegetable peeler, shave the carrots into thin ribbons. Slice the radishes thinly on a mandoline, and chop the cabbage. Combine all the ingredients in a large bowl with the Ginger-Almond Dressing and toss until thoroughly combined.

2. Serve as a side dish or as a main dish with the poultry, meat, or fish of your choice.

brussels sprouts salad
with bacon and pesto

serves 6 as a side

I have confessed many times my love of Brussels sprouts. I like to shave them into thin, crunchy ribbons to make a quick and easy salad or slaw. Even if you don't like Brussels sprouts, it's hard to resist them in a dressing of bacon and fresh pesto.

- 1 pound Brussels sprouts
- ½ cup Pesto (page 250)
- salt and pepper to taste
- 4 strips bacon, cooked and chopped
- 1 lemon, cut into wedges

1. With a mandoline on the thinnest setting, hold each Brussels sprout by the stem and slice until you reach the stem. Place the shaved Brussels sprouts in a medium-sized bowl along with the Pesto and salt and pepper and stir to combine.

2. Serve garnished with the chopped bacon, with lemon wedges on the side.

blistered grape tomato
stuffed portobello mushrooms

serves 3

Grape tomatoes are so much more enjoyable to me when they are roasted or blistered in some way, which tones down any gamey taste and sweetens them up quite a bit. I was combining them with mushrooms until I realized that it would be easier to stuff the mushrooms with the tomatoes and get it all done in one step.

- 3 portobello mushroom caps
- 2 tablespoons avocado oil, divided
- salt and pepper to taste
- ½ cup grape tomatoes
- 1 teaspoon minced fresh thyme
- 3 tablespoons crumbled goat cheese (optional)
- 2 tablespoons balsamic vinegar

1. Preheat the oven to 400°F and line a baking sheet with aluminum foil.

2. With a spoon, scrape out the gills and stems of the mushroom caps, then brush them with 1 tablespoon of the avocado oil and season with salt and pepper. Toss the grape tomatoes with the remaining avocado oil and thyme and season with salt and pepper.

3. Spread the mushroom caps scraped side down and the grape tomatoes on the foil-lined baking sheet, roast for 10 minutes, then flip the mushroom caps and roast for another 10 minutes.

4. Remove from the oven and stuff the grape tomatoes into the mushroom caps. Add the goat cheese, if using, then broil for 3 minutes.

5. Serve with a drizzle of balsamic vinegar over each stuffed mushroom.

roasted cauliflower salad
with pumpkin seeds

serves 4

It's hard not to love all things roasted, including vegetables. Roasting cauliflower brings out its natural sweetness and gives it a much richer flavor by letting it brown in the oven. Roasted cauliflower is great alone but is even more of an experience when mixed with a refreshing and tangy vinaigrette and served as a salad on a warm spring or summer day.

- 1 large head cauliflower, trimmed
- avocado oil for drizzling
- salt and pepper to taste
- 3 tablespoons pumpkin seeds
- 3 cups mixed greens
- ⅓ cup coarsely chopped fresh parsley
- 3 tablespoons extra-virgin olive oil
- 2½ tablespoons red wine vinegar

1. Preheat the oven to 400°F and line a baking sheet with aluminum foil.

2. Cut the cauliflower into uniform pieces and place on the foil-lined baking sheet. Drizzle with avocado oil, season with salt and pepper, and toss to coat. Roast for 25 minutes, shaking the pan halfway through. Remove from the oven and let cool for 15 minutes.

3. In a small pan over medium heat, toast the pumpkin seeds for 3 minutes, shaking the pan to prevent burning. Place the remaining ingredients in a large bowl, add the cauliflower and pumpkin seeds, and toss well to combine.

mixed green bean salad

I once preferred my green beans smothered in butter or roasted in lard, but my opinion changed when I saw these odd-looking purple string beans sitting in a basket at the farmers' market. I grabbed them and hauled them off with the intention to make a salad out of them. This salad is best as a side with fish or chicken because it works well with their subtle flavors.

- 1 pound green beans, stems trimmed
- ½ pound purple string beans, stems trimmed
- 3 tablespoons extra-virgin olive oil
- 2 tablespoons white wine vinegar
- 2 teaspoons brown mustard
- 1 shallot, thinly sliced
- 3 tablespoons chopped fresh parsley
- salt and pepper to taste

1. In a steamer basket over a pot of boiling water, steam the green and purple beans for 4 minutes, then plunge them into an ice water bath. When the beans are cool, drain the water and place them in a large bowl.

2. Combine the olive oil, vinegar, and mustard in a small bowl and whisk to combine. Pour the vinaigrette over the beans, add the shallot and parsley, season with salt and pepper, and toss well.

Note: You can use all green beans if you can't find purple string beans. The purple ones are more for appearance than taste.

seared brussels sprouts
with garlic and lemon

The title of this recipe may sound extravagant, but it's just the way I usually cook Brussels sprouts when I get a craving for them—which is quite often. So I decided to share an incredibly easy yet delicious way to make Brussels sprouts. That is, if you like Brussels sprouts; they say that your DNA determines whether you do. I'm glad that my DNA is working in my favor, because those who don't like them are truly missing out in my opinion.

- 2 tablespoons butter or ghee
- 1 pound Brussels sprouts, stemmed and sliced in half
- salt and pepper to taste
- 4 cloves garlic
- juice of ½ lemon

1. Heat the butter or ghee in a medium-sized pan over medium-high heat. Add the Brussels sprouts cut side down, then lower the heat to medium and cook for 4—5 minutes or until nicely charred on the cut side.

2. Season with salt and pepper, shake the pan, and cook for another 5 minutes. Grate the garlic and squeeze the lemon juice over the Brussels sprouts and toss again. Cook for 2 more minutes, tossing a couple of times, then serve.

cauliflower tabbouleh

Tabbouleh is a Levantine Arab salad made with a thicket of vibrant fresh parsley and mint and sweet tomatoes. Traditionally it's made with fresh cracked bulgur wheat. After reviewing the possibilities, I figured out that I could make it with cauliflower processed into a bulgur wheat–like consistency, with great success. We can now enjoy tabbouleh with a much-improved nutritional profile that's also gluten free.

- ½ head cauliflower
- 2 large bunches parsley
- 2 medium bunches mint
- 2 large tomatoes, chopped
- 1 shallot, minced
- juice of 1 lemon
- ⅓ cup extra-virgin olive oil
- ¼ teaspoon cinnamon
- ½ teaspoon allspice
- ¼ teaspoon pepper
- salt to taste
- romaine lettuce leaves for serving

1. With a coarse cheese grater, grate the cauliflower to a couscous-like consistency.

2. Combine all the ingredients in a large bowl and toss well. Serve on a bed of romaine lettuce leaves.

braised leeks and artichoke hearts

Braising isn't limited to meat; it's a great way to cook vegetables, too. The result is perfectly cooked and tender vegetables that contain much more concentrated flavors than an ordinary sauté. Here, fresh artichoke hearts and leeks are braised to tender bliss in fruity white wine and butter and finished with lemon and heavy cream for a creamy and piquant twist. The leeks and artichokes have such a unique and velvety mouthfeel when braised like this; everyone should try this dish at least once.

- 3 tablespoons butter
- 3 large leeks
- 4 artichoke hearts, quartered
- 3 cloves garlic
- 1 tablespoon chopped fresh thyme
- salt and pepper to taste
- ½ cup white wine
- ⅓ cup chicken Mother Stock (page 144)
- ¼ cup heavy cream
- juice of 1 lemon
- 1 tablespoon chopped fresh parsley

1. Preheat the oven to 325°F.

2. Heat the butter in a medium-sized Dutch oven or pot. Stir in the leeks, artichoke hearts, garlic, thyme, and salt and pepper and cook for 4 minutes or until the leeks begin to soften. Pour in the white wine and chicken stock, scraping the bottom of the pot. Bring to a simmer, reduce the heat to low, and simmer for 30 seconds.

3. Cover and transfer to the preheated oven for 35—40 minutes or until the artichoke hearts are easily pierced with a fork. Remove from the oven and add the heavy cream, lemon juice, and parsley. Stir to combine, then serve.

Note: If you're lactose intolerant, you can make this dish dairy free by substituting equal amounts of coconut oil and coconut milk for the butter and heavy cream, but doing so changes the flavor and consistency a lot.

ginger-lime coleslaw

I rarely eat out, partly because there aren't many restaurants I want to eat at. Revival Market in Houston is one exception because it serves fresh, pastured, grass-fed, and local cuisine that is beautifully prepared. I order the ginger-lime slaw almost every time because it's so alluring. The thought of each crunchy bite with its tart and slightly sweet, gingery finish always leads to this menu item appearing on my bill. This recipe is my attempt at replicating it. I think my version mimics the restaurant's quite well, but with my own flair.

- ¾ medium head purple cabbage, chopped
- 3 carrots, julienned
- 3 green onions, thinly sliced
- ½ cup Mayonnaise (page 252)
- juice of 3 limes
- 1-inch knob of ginger, peeled and grated
- 1 teaspoon Dijon mustard
- 1 tablespoon plus 1 teaspoon coconut aminos or tamari

1. In a large bowl, combine the cabbage, carrots, and green onions. In a smaller bowl, whisk together the Mayonnaise, lime juice, ginger, mustard, and coconut aminos or tamari.

2. Pour the dressing over the cabbage mixture and toss well.

vegetables

cucumber ribbon salad with creamy dill dressing

Combining creamy dill dressing and refreshing cucumbers, this salad makes an excellent side to a grilled or roasted main dish because it contrasts perfectly with the smokiness of the meat.

- ⅓ cup Mayonnaise (page 252)
- 2 cloves garlic, grated
- 2 tablespoons lemon juice
- 1½ tablespoons chopped fresh dill
- 2 English cucumbers
- salt and pepper to taste

1. Mix the Mayonnaise, garlic, lemon juice, and dill in a small bowl until well combined.

2. With a vegetable peeler, shave the cucumbers into thin ribbons, and place them in a large bowl.

3. Add the dressing to the shaved cucumbers and toss to combine. Season with salt and pepper and serve.

spaghetti squash alfredo with mushrooms

Most people appreciate a nice alfredo. Why not make it with spaghetti squash? Not only is it healthier than pasta, but I think it's better, because spaghetti squash, unlike pasta, actually tastes like something. The squash imparts a slight sweetness to this creamy dish, which balances the flavors excellently and takes Italian to a whole new level.

- 1 spaghetti squash, cut in half lengthwise and seeds removed
- avocado oil for brushing (if not using a pressure cooker)
- 3 tablespoons butter or ghee
- 2 cloves garlic, minced
- 1 shallot, minced
- 8 ounces (about 2 cups) cremini mushrooms, sliced
- ½ cup heavy cream or coconut milk
- 7 basil leaves
- ½ cup grated Parmesan cheese (optional)

1. If you have a pressure cooker, fill it with ¾ cup water and place an elevated steamer basket in the bottom. Place the spaghetti squash halves in the steamer basket and cook on high for 8 minutes. If you do not have a pressure cooker, brush the cut sides of the squash with avocado oil, place on a baking sheet, and roast in a 400°F oven for 45–50 minutes or until easily pierced with a fork.

2. Once your spaghetti squash is cooked, scrape out the insides with a fork. Heat the butter or ghee in a medium-sized pan over medium heat, add the garlic and shallot, and cook until the shallot is soft, about 4 minutes.

3. Add the mushrooms and cook for 5–6 minutes, stirring occasionally, then pour in the heavy cream or coconut milk while scraping the bottom of the pan. Add the spaghetti squash, season with salt and pepper, and stir until thoroughly coated. Simmer in the sauce for 3 minutes, then remove from the heat.

4. Roll up the basil leaves in the shape of a cigar, slice thinly, and sprinkle over the Spaghetti Squash Alfredo, along with the Parmesan, if using. Stir once more and serve.

grilled zucchini with tzatziki sauce

I have an obsession with grilling during the summer. I can't help it; the season seems to grab hold of me and control my every movement. Plus, I'm pretty sure that grilling qualifies as a sport in Texas, which might be another driving force. Grilled zucchini is wonderful, but it's even better when it's smothered in a tart and refreshing tzatziki sauce and garnished with fresh parsley.

- 2 large zucchini, cut into ½-inch slices
- 1 tablespoon avocado oil
- salt and pepper to taste
- ¼ cup chopped fresh parsley
- Tzatziki Sauce for serving (page 251)

1. Preheat a gas grill to medium-high heat. Brush each zucchini slice on both sides with avocado oil and season with salt and pepper.

2. Grill the zucchini slices for 4—5 minutes per side or until tender. While the zucchini grills, assemble the Tzatziki Sauce and keep cold.

3. Serve the zucchini with a sprinkle of parsley and pepper and Tzatziki Sauce for dipping.

cauliflower tortillas

If you've been to my blog, you may notice that this recipe comes directly from there. I couldn't help but add it to the book because it has been so incredibly popular, pinned well over 100,000 times on Pinterest and linked to all over the Internet. While I'm thrilled with that recognition, I have no idea why it exploded so much, other than that it's a tortilla substitute made from cauliflower. These cauliflower tortillas work equally well as wraps or even as lasagna "noodles."

- ¾ head cauliflower
- 2 eggs
- salt and pepper to taste

1. Preheat the oven to 375°F and line a baking sheet with parchment paper.

2. Trim the cauliflower, cut it into small, uniform pieces, and pulse in a food processor in batches until you get a couscous-like consistency. The finely riced cauliflower should make about 2 cups packed.

3. Place the cauliflower in a microwave-safe bowl and microwave for 2 minutes, then stir and microwave again for another 2 minutes. Place the cauliflower in a fine cheesecloth or dishtowel and squeeze out as much water as possible, being careful not to burn yourself. I suggest wearing dishwashing gloves, as it is usually very hot.

4. In a medium bowl, whisk the eggs. Add the cauliflower and mix until combined. Spread the mixture onto the baking sheet in 6 circles, each about ½-inch thick.

5. Bake for 10 minutes, carefully flip each cauliflower tortilla, and return to the oven for another 5–7 minutes or until completely set. Place the tortillas on a wire rack to cool slightly, about 4 minutes.

6. Heat a medium-sized skillet on medium heat. Place a tortilla in the pan, pressing down slightly, and brown for 1–2 minutes per side or until the desired doneness is achieved. Repeat with the remaining tortillas.

garlic-dijon spinach with pine nuts

serves 3

Spinach is pretty undeniable to me with a little bit of lemon juice and garlic, but, like many simple recipes, it can get old over time. I like to switch between that preparation and this recipe to keep things interesting. Here I coat tender wilted spinach in slightly sweet and tangy Dijon mustard and top it with irresistibly smoky toasted pine nuts.

- ¼ cup pine nuts
- 2 tablespoons butter or ghee
- 3 cloves garlic, minced
- 5 ounces spinach
- 2 tablespoons Dijon mustard
- salt and pepper to taste

1. In a small pan over medium heat, toast the pine nuts for about 4 minutes or until lightly browned and fragrant, shaking the pan often to prevent burning. Pour onto a plate to cool.

2. Heat the butter or ghee in a medium-sized pan over medium heat. Add the garlic and sauté for about 30 seconds, then stir in the spinach. Cook for 3—4 minutes, stirring occasionally, until completely wilted, then stir in the mustard and season with salt and pepper.

3. Serve the spinach garnished with the toasted pine nuts.

roasted cabbage wedges with cilantro-lime vinaigrette

Cabbage is an overlooked and misunderstood vegetable. When people hear the word *cabbage*, they often turn up their noses in disgust. I have concluded that most of the people who have that reaction have probably never eaten cabbage that was cooked properly. Cabbage has many uses and works well to absorb almost any flavor. In this recipe, tender and crisp-edged cabbage wedges are coated with a vibrant and refreshing vinaigrette. It's a quick and easy side dish that makes a wonderful presentation for a get-together or a simple weeknight meal.

for the cabbage:

- 1 head cabbage, white or green, cut into 6 wedges
- 1½ tablespoons avocado oil
- salt and pepper to taste

for the vinaigrette:

- ⅓ cup olive oil
- 1 teaspoon Dijon mustard
- 2 tablespoons chopped fresh cilantro
- zest and juice of 1 lime

1. Preheat the oven to 400°F.

2. Brush both sides of the cabbage wedges with the avocado oil and season with salt and pepper. Place the wedges on a baking sheet and roast for 20 minutes, then flip each wedge and continue cooking for 20−25 more minutes or until tender and lightly browned.

3. In a small bowl, whisk all the vinaigrette ingredients until well combined.

4. Serve the cabbage wedges with the vinaigrette spooned on top.

green beans with
butter-toasted almonds

serves 4—5

This is one of my mom's classic recipes. She is an incredibly resourceful and inquisitive chef, and by that I mean she uses copious amounts of butter and garlic in her food. What can I say, though? I tend to do the same thing; I suppose it's in my blood. This recipe combines blistered green beans with almonds that are slowly toasted in bubbling butter. It makes a simple yet elegant side dish.

- 2 tablespoons butter or ghee, divided
- 1 pound green beans, stems trimmed
- salt and pepper to taste
- ⅓ cup chopped almonds

1. In a medium-sized pan, heat 1 tablespoon of the butter or ghee over medium heat, then add the green beans and season with salt and pepper. Cover and cook for 3 minutes, then shake the pan, cover, and cook for another 4 minutes. Reduce the heat to low and continue cooking for 3—4 more minutes or until tender.

2. Heat the remaining 1 tablespoon butter or ghee in a small skillet over medium heat. When the butter begins to bubble, add the chopped almonds and stir to coat them evenly. Reduce the heat to medium-low and toast the almonds in the butter for about 2 minutes or until they begin to brown.

3. Serve the green beans with the butter-toasted almonds on top.

loaded cauliflower mash

serves 5

I created this recipe with a loaded baked potato in mind. Having been raised by a Southern mother, I find it just plain wrong to turn down a loaded baked potato, so I made one, but in mash form, with the twist of using cauliflower. Cauliflower adds a slight sweetness that you don't get from potatoes, along with a slightly smoother and creamier texture. And of course there's bacon.

- 1 head cauliflower, trimmed and chopped into florets
- 1 tablespoon butter or ghee
- salt and pepper to taste
- 5 strips bacon, cooked and chopped
- 2 tablespoons chopped fresh chives
- grated Gruyère cheese (optional)

1. If you have a pressure cooker, place the cauliflower florets in an elevated steamer basket and cook at high pressure for 4 minutes, then release the pressure by using the quick-release method. If you do not have a pressure cooker, simply steam the cauliflower in a steamer basket over boiling water for 10 minutes or until soft.

2. Place the cooked cauliflower in a food processor or blender with the butter or ghee and season with salt and pepper. Process until smooth.

3. Fill a serving bowl with the cauliflower mash and stir in the cooked bacon pieces, chives, and Gruyère, if using.

—— desserts and sweets ——

lemon poppy seed loaf

makes 1 loaf

On my blog, slimpalate.com, I posted a recipe for Lemon Chia Seed Muffins—a unique rendition of the classic lemon poppy seed muffin. I really loved their texture, but I was never fully satisfied with them because using chia seeds instead of poppy seeds altered the original recipe too much. I also felt that the recipe was better suited to loaf form. The result was this moist, slightly tart, and lemony loaf, a light-tasting treat that is perfect with a cup of coffee or tea.

- ½ cup coconut flour, sifted
- 2 tablespoons poppy seeds
- ¼ teaspoon baking soda
- pinch of salt
- 4 eggs
- ½ cup honey or ½ teaspoon liquid stevia mixed with ½ cup unsweetened almond milk
- 2 tablespoons lemon juice
- 2 tablespoons lemon zest
- ¼ cup coconut oil, melted, plus extra for greasing the pan
- 1 tablespoon apple cider vinegar
- ½ teaspoon pure vanilla extract

1. Preheat the oven to 350°F and grease a small loaf pan with coconut oil.

2. In a medium-sized bowl, add the coconut flour, poppy seeds, baking soda, and salt and stir to combine. In a separate bowl, whisk together the eggs, honey or stevia with almond milk, lemon juice and zest, coconut oil, vinegar, and vanilla.

3. Pour the wet ingredients into the dry ingredients and stir until thoroughly incorporated, then pour into the greased loaf pan. Bake for 45–50 minutes or until a toothpick inserted in the center comes out clean.

4. Carefully remove the loaf from the pan and let cool on a wire rack for at least 10 minutes before slicing and serving.

raspberry meringue tarts

I don't bake much, nor do I make many pies, but when I'm in the mood, I like to make tarts. I prefer tarts because they are smaller and, to be honest, just so undeniably adorable. They are also a great change of pace for me since I usually eat some form of chocolate as a treat. These tarts are made with a fresh raspberry curd and topped with a torched meringue frosting, making them excellent desserts to display and serve at a party or deliver as gifts.

for the crust:

- 2 cups blanched almond flour
- 1 tablespoon coconut flour, sifted
- pinch of salt
- 1 egg
- 1 tablespoon honey or 5 drops liquid stevia
- 2 tablespoons lard, melted, plus more for greasing the tart pans

for the raspberry curd:

- 3 cups raspberries
- 4 teaspoons lemon juice
- zest of 1 lemon
- ¼ cup honey or ¼ teaspoon liquid stevia mixed with ¼ cup water
- 4 egg yolks
- 2 tablespoons plus 1½ teaspoons arrowroot starch

for the meringue:

- 2 tablespoons honey or 8 drops liquid stevia
- 2 egg whites
- ¼ teaspoon lemon juice

1. Preheat the oven to 350°F and grease four 4-inch tart pans with lard.

2. In a medium-sized bowl, combine the almond flour, coconut flour, and salt. In a separate bowl, whisk together the egg and honey or stevia. Pour the wet ingredients into the dry ingredients and mix, then add the melted lard and continue mixing until well incorporated.

3. Divide the dough into 4 equal portions and press into the tart pans. Bake for 10 minutes or until lightly browned around the edges. Let cool for 10 minutes.

4. In a blender, purée the raspberries until smooth. Press through a mesh sieve and discard the seeds. In a medium-sized bowl, combine the raspberry puree, lemon juice and zest, and honey or stevia with water. In a small bowl, whisk the egg yolks, then pour the egg yolks into the raspberry mixture and mix until well combined. Pour into a medium-sized saucepan over medium heat, stir to combine, then whisk in the arrowroot starch in batches to avoid clumps. Continue whisking until the mixture is slightly less thick than honey, 1–2 minutes. Then divide the raspberry curd evenly among the crusts and refrigerate for 1 hour or until cool and set.

5. Once the tarts have set, make the meringue. Heat the honey (skip this step if using stevia) in a small saucepan over medium heat until bubbling, then reduce the heat to medium-low. In a bowl, beat the egg whites on high until frothy, then add the lemon juice and continue beating on high until stiff peaks form. While continuing to beat on high, slowly pour the hot honey or stevia down the side of the bowl and beat it into the mixture. Continue beating on high for about 4 minutes to maintain stiff peaks. Pipe or spoon the meringue evenly onto each tart, then brown the tops lightly with a kitchen torch or under the broiler.

mocha cupcakes with
roasted hazelnut—chocolate frosting

makes 9—10 cupcakes

This recipe is essentially a homemade version of coffee cupcakes with Nutella frosting. When I was making "homemade Nutella" with fresh roasted hazelnuts and cacao powder (see my recipe on page 256), I couldn't help but think that it would make an excellent frosting. I believe my cupcakes are better than store-bought because they're made with fresh ingredients, and nothing trumps fresh ingredients.

- 1½ cups plus 3 tablespoons hazelnuts

for the cupcakes:

- ½ cup coconut flour, sifted
- ½ cup unsweetened cacao powder
- ½ teaspoon baking soda
- pinch of salt
- 4 eggs
- 2 teaspoons pure vanilla extract
- ½ cup honey or ½ teaspoon liquid stevia mixed with ½ cup unsweetened almond milk
- ½ cup strong cold-brew coffee
- ¼ cup unsalted butter or ghee, melted

for the frosting:

- 4 ounces 85% dark chocolate, chopped
- ½ teaspoon pure vanilla extract
- ¼ teaspoon salt
- 10 drops liquid stevia or 1 tablespoon honey
- 4 tablespoons plus 1 teaspoon water

Note: Cold-brew coffee can be found at grocery stores like Whole Foods. I use Chameleon Cold-Brew.

1. Preheat the oven to 375°F and line a baking sheet with parchment paper.

2. Place the hazelnuts on the parchment-lined baking sheet and roast for 10 minutes, shaking the pan halfway through to prevent burning. Pull the hazelnuts out of the oven and lower the temperature to 350°F. Place the hazelnuts in a clean dishtowel and rub vigorously to remove the skins.

3. Set aside 3 tablespoons of the roasted hazelnuts and put the rest in a food processor or blender. Pulse and process, scraping the sides occasionally, until it turns into a smooth nut butter. This step can take up to 10 minutes depending on how powerful your food processor or blender is.

4. Grease a muffin pan or line it with baking cups. In a medium-sized bowl, combine the coconut flour, cacao powder, baking soda, and salt and mix with a fork to combine. In a separate bowl, whisk together the eggs, vanilla, honey or stevia with almond milk, and coffee. Pour the wet ingredients into the dry ingredients and stir until thoroughly incorporated, then mix in the melted butter or ghee. Fill the baking cups two-thirds full with the batter and bake for 20—25 minutes or until an inserted toothpick comes out clean. Place the cupcakes on a wire rack to cool completely.

5. While the cupcakes cool, make the frosting. Melt the chocolate in a double boiler, stirring to prevent burning. In a medium-sized bowl, add the hazelnut butter, melted chocolate, vanilla, and salt and stir to combine, then stir in the stevia or honey. Refrigerate for 15—25 minutes to thicken and set. With a hand blender, whip the frosting thoroughly, then add the water while whipping until well incorporated.

6. Chop the reserved hazelnuts and frost the cupcakes, then sprinkle the chopped hazelnuts on top. Store on a covered cake stand for up to 4 days or in the fridge for up to 2 weeks.

salted dark chocolate
almond butter fudge

Along with ice cream, chocolate is one of my favorite sweets—especially if it's salted chocolate. A sprinkle of crunchy, flaky sea salt transforms chocolate into a much more immersive experience. To take that experience even further, this salted chocolate comes in the form of smooth and chewy fudge with a deep, dark chocolate flavor.

- 1 cup almond butter
- ⅓ cup coconut oil, softened
- ½ cup unsweetened cacao powder
- 1 teaspoon pure vanilla extract
- 20 drops liquid stevia or 3 tablespoons honey
- flaky or coarse sea salt for sprinkling

1. Line a small loaf pan with parchment paper.

2. In a medium-sized bowl, combine the almond butter, coconut oil, cacao powder, vanilla, and stevia or honey. Mix until thoroughly incorporated and no clumps remain.

3. Pour the mixture into the parchment-lined loaf pan and generously sprinkle with sea salt. Freeze for 45 minutes or until the mixture has set.

4. Carefully pull out the block of fudge, cut into 1-inch squares, and serve immediately. Store any leftover fudge in the freezer.

Note: After pulling this fudge out of the freezer, I usually let it sit out for 5–10 minutes to soften up a bit before serving or eating.

cardamom and pistachio
chocolate truffles

makes 25—30 truffles

Smooth and creamy ganache made with coconut milk and rolled in toasted pistachios is one of my favorite chocolate treats because of its velvety richness. Even though these truffles are dairy free, which makes them suitable for those who are lactose intolerant, they are just as good as the ones made with butter, and that's saying something.

- 8 ounces dark chocolate (70% or higher), chopped
- 3 tablespoons coconut oil
- ½ teaspoon pure vanilla extract
- pinch of salt
- 1 cup coconut milk
- 6 cardamom pods
- 1 cup pistachios

1. Place the chocolate, coconut oil, vanilla, and salt in a medium-sized bowl. Pour the coconut milk into a small saucepan over medium heat, add the cardamom pods, and heat until steaming, stirring constantly. Turn off the burner, cover, and let steep for at least 10 minutes and up to 30 minutes.

2. In a medium-sized pan over medium heat, toast the pistachios, tossing to prevent burning, until lightly browned and fragrant, 4—5 minutes.

3. Reheat the coconut milk until hot and steamy again, then pour through a mesh sieve over the chocolate mixture in the bowl, pressing on the cardamom pods to extract all the flavor. Let the mixture sit for 1 minute, then gently whisk until thoroughly blended and completely smooth. Pour the mixture into a small loaf pan, cover with plastic wrap, and refrigerate for 2—3 hours or overnight.

4. Line a baking sheet with parchment paper. Coarsely chop the toasted pistachios, then place them on a plate for rolling. With a melon baller, scoop out and form 1-inch balls of the ganache and place them on the parchment-lined baking sheet. Refrigerate for 30 minutes. Roll the chilled balls in the chopped pistachios and serve immediately, or store in an airtight container in the fridge for up to 2 weeks.

Notes: I prefer using chocolate that contains 70–85% cacao. Anything lower would result in too soft a ganache, and anything higher might not be sweet enough.

If your chocolate mixture has a grainy appearance, it has "broken." You can save it by slowly stirring in drops of hot water until it is smooth again.

pumpkin blondies

When fall comes around, I tend to use a lot of pumpkin. Inevitably I end up exploiting the poor squash. Pumpkin is incredibly versatile in cooking and baking and makes a wonderful bread or cake. The warmly spiced fragrance of these blondies always calls people to the kitchen to ask what's in the oven. When the blondies make their way out of the oven, I like to put a pat of butter on them and toast them in a pan.

- butter or ghee for greasing the pan
- ¼ cup coconut flour, sifted
- ½ cup blanched almond flour
- pinch of salt
- ½ cup crushed walnuts
- 1 teaspoon cinnamon
- ½ teaspoon baking soda
- 2 eggs
- ⅓ cup honey or ½ teaspoon liquid stevia mixed with ⅓ cup unsweetened almond milk or coconut milk
- 1 teaspoon pure vanilla extract
- 1 cup pumpkin puree

1. Preheat the oven to 350°F and grease an 8x8-inch baking pan with butter or ghee.

2. In a medium-sized bowl, mix together the coconut flour, almond flour, salt, walnuts, cinnamon, and baking soda. In a separate bowl, whisk together the eggs, honey or stevia with almond or coconut milk, and vanilla, then whisk in the pumpkin puree until well distributed. Pour the wet ingredients into the dry ingredients and mix until thoroughly incorporated.

3. Spread the batter into the greased baking pan. Bake for 35−40 minutes or until a toothpick inserted in the center comes out clean. Let cool, then slice into 12 bars.

brownies

I used to think that it would be impossible to make a grain-free brownie that was slightly chewy and tasted like an "actual" brownie. Then I realized that it isn't the flour that makes a brownie great, but a healthy amount of butter. It really doesn't get much better than brownie batter consisting of almost half butter. Using that amount of butter keeps the brownies moist and decadently chewy and rich: my best brownie recipe ever, thanks to the power of butter.

- 3 ounces unsweetened baking chocolate, chopped
- ½ cup unsalted butter, plus more for greasing the pan
- ¼ cup coconut flour, sifted
- ¼ teaspoon baking soda
- pinch of salt
- 2 eggs
- 1 teaspoon pure vanilla extract
- ½ cup honey or ½ teaspoon liquid stevia mixed with ½ cup unsweetened almond milk

1. Preheat the oven to 350°F and grease an 8x8-inch baking pan with butter.

2. In a double boiler, melt the chocolate, stirring to make sure it doesn't burn. When the chocolate is melted, slice the butter into 1-inch cubes and mix it into the melted chocolate until fully incorporated, then remove from the heat.

3. In a medium-sized bowl, thoroughly combine the coconut flour, baking soda, and salt. In a smaller bowl, whisk together the eggs, vanilla, and honey or stevia with almond milk. Pour the egg mixture into the dry ingredients and stir to combine, making sure no clumps remain, then continue stirring for 30 more seconds. Pour in the melted chocolate and stir again to thoroughly incorporate.

4. Pour the batter into the greased baking pan and bake for 25–30 minutes or until a toothpick inserted in the center comes out clean. Let the brownies cool for at least 15 minutes, then slice into 12 bars.

mexican chocolate chocolate cookies

makes 12–16 cookies

I knew I wanted to come up with a Mexican chocolate recipe when I started having incessant dreams about the velvety Mexican hot chocolate that my cousin Jenny had described to me and eventually showed me how to make. Then I thought to myself, Why stop at liquid form? Why not take it to a solid level—like a cookie? And no, the redundant use of the word *chocolate* in the recipe title is not a mistake. I was simply trying to convey the double chocolaty-ness as accurately as possible. You could say it's so chocolaty that you have to say *chocolate* twice.

- 1 cup blanched almond flour
- 1 tablespoon coconut flour, sifted
- 4 ounces dark chocolate (70% or higher), chopped
- ½ cup unsweetened cacao powder
- ½ teaspoon chipotle chili powder
- 2 teaspoons cinnamon
- ¼ teaspoon nutmeg
- ¼ teaspoon baking soda
- pinch of salt
- 1 egg
- ¼ cup butter, softened, or coconut oil, melted
- 2 teaspoons pure vanilla extract
- ¼ cup honey or ½ teaspoon liquid stevia mixed with ¼ cup unsweetened almond milk

1. Preheat the oven to 350°F and line a baking sheet with parchment paper.

2. In a medium-sized bowl, add the almond flour, coconut flour, chocolate, cacao powder, chipotle chili powder, cinnamon, nutmeg, baking soda, and salt and mix thoroughly with a fork.

3. In a small bowl, add the egg, butter or coconut oil, vanilla, and honey or stevia with almond milk and whisk until well combined. Stir the wet ingredients into the dry ingredients.

4. Spoon heaping tablespoons of batter onto the parchment-lined baking sheet, evenly spaced. Bake for 15–20 minutes or until the cookies are soft with a light spring in the center.

5. Once the cookies are cool enough to handle, place them on a wire rack for 5 minutes to finish cooling.

coconut macaroons

There is a distinct difference between macaroons and French macarons. Macaroons, the cookies you are making in this recipe, typically contain coconut. French macarons are made with sugar and almond flour and are known for their pretty and colorful appearance. Both are fabulous, but these cookies are much easier to make. They have a crispy exterior and a light, chewy interior, and they make wonderful gifts for those who like coconut. (To my surprise, many people do not, which I find very sad.)

- 3 egg whites
- ¼ cup honey or ¼ teaspoon liquid stevia mixed with ¼ cup unsweetened almond milk
- ½ teaspoon pure vanilla extract
- ¼ teaspoon salt
- 3 cups unsweetened shredded coconut

1. Preheat the oven to 350°F and line a baking sheet with parchment paper.

2. In a medium-sized bowl, whisk the egg whites, honey or stevia with almond milk, vanilla, and salt until frothy. Fold in the coconut until fully incorporated and no dry clumps remain.

3. Using your hands or a cookie scoop, form the mixture into heaping tablespoons about 1½ inches in diameter and drop onto the parchment-lined baking sheet, evenly spaced.

4. Bake for 15—20 minutes or until golden brown on the tops and bottoms. Let cool on a wire rack for at least 15 minutes. Store in the fridge for up to a week and a half.

Note: For a fun variation, dip the bottoms of the macaroons in melted chocolate and let it solidify before serving.

coconut butter—stuffed cinnamon cookie sandwiches

makes 8—9 sandwiches

Sometimes I make a type of snickerdoodle cookie without the sugar coating. Because it lacks that sugar coating, it's technically not a snickerdoodle. To make up for that, I stuff creamy coconut butter between two cookies, making cookie sandwiches. Each bite of chewy cookie and oozing coconut butter is a dense and satisfying treat even without the sugar.

- 2 cups blanched almond flour
- 2 tablespoons coconut flour, sifted
- ¼ teaspoon baking soda
- ¼ teaspoon salt
- 1 egg
- 1 teaspoon pure vanilla extract
- ¼ cup coconut oil, melted
- ¼ cup honey or ½ teaspoon liquid stevia mixed with ¼ cup unsweetened almond milk
- 2 tablespoons cinnamon
- ¼ cup coconut butter

1. Preheat the oven to 350°F and line a baking sheet with parchment paper.

2. In a medium-sized bowl, combine the almond flour, coconut flour, baking soda, and salt. In a separate bowl, whisk together the egg, vanilla, coconut oil, and honey or stevia with almond milk, then pour the wet mixture into the dry mixture and mix until thoroughly incorporated.

3. Form the dough into balls about 1-inch in diameter. Roll them in the cinnamon, then place them on the baking sheet. With the bottom of a glass or a mason jar, carefully press down on the dough balls to flatten them to ½-inch thickness. Bake for 15—20 minutes or until the cookies are set and have a slight resistance to the touch. Let cool on a wire rack for about 15 minutes.

4. Melt the coconut butter in the warm oven until pourable, then stuff about a teaspoon between 2 cookies. Repeat with the remaining cookies. Let the cookie sandwiches solidify at room temperature before serving, or store in the refrigerator for up to 2 weeks.

Note: Coconut butter is not the same as coconut oil. It can be purchased at most grocery stores, such as Whole Foods.

strawberry and toasted vanilla bean ice cream

When my friend Izy taught me that you can toast and use whole vanilla beans in recipes, it started me dreaming about the many possibilities. Here, combining the intense flavor of toasted vanilla beans with fresh strawberry puree and creamy coconut milk makes a simple yet distinguished ice cream.

- 2 vanilla bean pods
- 2 (13.5-ounce) cans coconut milk
- ½ cup honey
- 1 teaspoon gelatin
- 3 egg yolks
- 13 ounces strawberries (about 3 cups), hulled
- 1 tablespoon potato vodka or kirsch (optional)
- pinch of sea salt

1. In a small pan over medium heat, toast the vanilla bean pods, tossing to prevent burning, for 2–3 minutes or until fragrant, then grind them into a powder with a mortar and pestle or spice grinder.

2. In a medium-sized saucepan, warm the coconut milk and honey, then whisk in the gelatin and vanilla bean powder. In a small bowl, whisk the egg yolks. Whisk a little bit of the warm coconut milk mixture into the egg yolks, then add the egg yolk mixture to the coconut milk mixture and whisk until it has slightly thickened and coats the back of a spoon. Strain the mixture through a mesh sieve into a large bowl and refrigerate until thoroughly chilled, preferably overnight.

3. Purée the strawberries in a blender until smooth. Add the strawberry puree, potato vodka or kirsch (if using), and salt to the chilled mixture and mix until well combined. Pour into an ice cream maker and churn and freeze according to the manufacturer's directions.

4. Serve the ice cream immediately, or transfer it to a freezer-safe container and keep it in the freezer until ready to serve. If freezing and serving later, let it sit out for 10 minutes to soften before serving.

Note: The optional alcohol makes the ice cream softer and keeps it from becoming hard when stored in the freezer. However, it is not required for the recipe. If you prefer not to use it, simply pull the ice cream out of the freezer and let it sit at room temperature for an additional 10 minutes to soften it up and make it easier to scoop.

mint-avocado ice cream with cacao nibs

I've always been indecisive when it comes to choosing a favorite ice cream flavor, but mint is one of my favorites. The problem was that every time I tried to make it at home with mint extract, the extract gave it a slight taste of alcohol. So I made this version with fresh mint that steeps in creamy coconut milk, infusing it with mint flavor. This preparation creates a much more deeply flavored and vibrant ice cream, with a nice crunch from the espresso-flavored cacao nibs. If you're put off by the slightly odd-sounding idea of using avocados in ice cream, I assure you that they are hardly noticeable; they give it a wonderful creamy texture and a slightly green color to match the refreshing mint.

- 2 (13.5-ounce) cans coconut milk
- 2 bunches mint (about 2 cups packed)
- ½ cup honey or ½ teaspoon liquid stevia
- 2 avocados
- pinch of salt
- 1 teaspoon potato vodka (optional)
- ½ cup unsweetened cacao nibs

1. Heat the coconut milk, mint, and honey or stevia in a medium-sized saucepan, stirring until hot and steamy. Turn off the heat, cover, and let steep for 45 minutes.

2. Halve the avocados, remove the pits, scrape out the flesh, and place in a food processor or blender along with the salt and potato vodka, if using. Pour the coconut milk mixture through a mesh strainer into the food processor or blender, pressing the mint against the strainer to squeeze out as much flavor as possible. Process until completely smooth, then refrigerate for at least 2 hours or overnight.

3. Churn and freeze the mixture in an ice cream maker according to the manufacturer's directions. Once the ice cream begins to reach the desired consistency, add the cacao nibs. Serve immediately or store in the freezer in a plastic or metal container.

sauces, dressings, and dips

french vinaigrette

The French know their cuisine, even their salads. My French vinaigrette closely resembles a classic French vinaigrette, but with a little more tartness. I prefer my vinaigrettes on the tart side, with equal parts vinegar and extra-virgin olive oil. It's the slight acidity that makes you want to go back for another refreshing bite.

- ⅓ cup extra-virgin olive oil
- ⅓ cup red wine vinegar
- 1½ teaspoons Dijon mustard
- 1 shallot, minced

1. In a small bowl, whisk the olive oil, red wine vinegar, Dijon mustard, and shallot until thoroughly combined.

2. Let sit for 3—4 minutes and whisk again before serving.

lemon-garlic vinaigrette

People talk about how garlic breath is so embarrassing, but I say embrace it! Garlic breath is a badge of honor that says you don't care what anyone else thinks because you just had a delicious meal that everyone would be jealous of. Garlic is one of those things that, though pungent in odor, makes things taste incredible. A generous amount of fresh-grated garlic gives this vinaigrette a powerful finish on a salad or as a dipping sauce.

- ½ cup extra-virgin olive oil
- ⅓ cup lemon juice
- 2 teaspoons whole-grain mustard
- 2 cloves garlic, grated

1. In a small bowl, whisk together all the ingredients. Use immediately or store in the fridge.

ginger-almond dressing

In this recipe I replaced peanut butter with almond butter in an attempt to re-create an old favorite. I have always loved the classic peanut dressings at Asian restaurants; even when I didn't like vegetables, I would dunk everything other than vegetables into it. Now that I have a much wider appreciation for food, I still crave that sweet, nutty, umami-packed flavor. You don't have to use this dressing on a salad; it also works wonderfully as a dipping sauce for grilled or tandoori-style meats.

- ½ cup almond butter
- 1½ tablespoons coconut aminos or tamari
- 1 tablespoon unseasoned rice vinegar
- 2 tablespoons water
- 1 tablespoon fish sauce
- 1-inch knob of ginger, peeled and grated
- 2 cloves garlic, grated

1. Combine all the ingredients a medium-sized bowl. Serve immediately or store in the fridge for up to 3 weeks.

barbecue sauce

Although I use barbecue sauce very selectively, and only when I'm in the mood for it, not liking barbecue sauce is considered a sin in my family. I prefer to make mine with a base of onion and vinegar for a slightly tart and sweet sauce that isn't too runny.

- 2 tablespoons macadamia nut oil or avocado oil
- ½ medium onion, finely chopped
- 3 cloves garlic, thinly sliced
- 2 tablespoons tomato paste
- ½ teaspoon cinnamon
- 1 teaspoon mustard powder
- 1 teaspoon ground cumin
- 2 teaspoons chipotle chili powder
- ¼ cup apple cider vinegar
- ¼ cup water
- 6 drops liquid stevia or 2 teaspoons honey

1. In a medium-sized pan, heat the oil over medium heat. Add the onion and garlic and sauté for 4–5 minutes or until softened. Add the tomato paste and stir until thoroughly combined, then add the cinnamon, mustard powder, cumin, and chipotle chili powder and cook for 2 minutes, stirring frequently to prevent burning.

2. Add the vinegar and water, scraping the bottom of the pan, then pour the mixture into a blender along with the stevia or honey and purée until smooth. Store in the fridge for up to 3 weeks.

pesto

makes about ½ cup

Pesto has a special place in my heart thanks to my brother, Nick. When I was growing up, I despised pesto for no known reason really—that is, until my brother said that he loved it. Of course, I had to be just like him and love it, too. That change in mindset gave me a more positive outlook the next time I tried pesto, and I ended up falling in love with it. I honestly think it happened because I took a moment to really taste the fragrant notes of basil, the smooth flavor of olive oil, and the slight bite of garlic working together.

- ¼ cup walnuts
- 2 cups loosely packed fresh basil
- ½ cup loosely packed grated Parmesan cheese (optional)
- 5 cloves garlic
- ½ cup extra-virgin olive oil
- salt to taste

1. In a food processor, combine the walnuts, basil, Parmesan cheese (if using), and garlic and process until smooth.

2. Add the olive oil and salt and process again until smooth and well mixed. Serve immediately or store in the fridge for up to 1 week.

tzatziki sauce

Greek food is one of those cuisines that I consider to be soul food—food that is good for your soul. My parents took me to Greek restaurants all the time when I was a kid. We loaded up on pita back then, but even without the bread, you can still enjoy Greek classics like tzatziki sauce. Tzatziki is traditionally used as a sauce for gyros, but it can also be used on other meat dishes like kebabs and roasts. Its light and refreshing taste works well with a fatty, salty meat to help cut the richness.

- ½ medium cucumber, peeled
- 1 cup plain full-fat yogurt
- 2 cloves garlic, minced
- 1½ tablespoons extra-virgin olive oil
- 1 tablespoon red wine vinegar
- 4 mint leaves, thinly sliced
- salt to taste

1. Grate the cucumber with a coarse grater into a medium-sized bowl. Add the rest of the ingredients and stir until well incorporated.

2. Refrigerate and serve chilled. This sauce can be made up to 3 days ahead of time and kept covered in the fridge.

mayonnaise

For the longest time, I thought that mayonnaise was unhealthy and that eating it would end my life. Now, if it's store-bought mayonnaise made with sugar, rancid vegetable oil, and soy, then it might. But if it's made at home with fresh egg yolks and healthful oils, then I don't see a problem with it. Homemade mayonnaise is much more flavorful than store-bought, with too many uses to count. You can use this mayonnaise by itself, mix it into a sauce, use it as a binder or as a component of an aioli, and much more. Not to mention that a little trick I learned from one of my favorite cooking sites, Serious Eats, makes it twice as fast and easy to prepare.

- 1 egg yolk
- 2 tablespoons lemon juice
- 1 teaspoon water
- 1½ teaspoons Dijon mustard
- salt to taste
- 1 cup macadamia nut oil or avocado oil

1. Place the egg yolk, lemon juice, water, mustard, and salt in a tall, flat-bottomed glass or an immersion blender cup large enough to fit the base of a hand blender.

2. Insert a hand blender or immersion blender and touch it to the bottom of the cup. Slowly pour in the oil to minimize the mixing of the rest of the ingredients. Blend, holding the blender against the bottom, until the ingredients are fully emulsified.

3. Mayonnaise can be stored in the fridge for 1—2 weeks.

roasted tomatillo salsa

Tomatillos are smaller, green-colored tomatoes that have a slightly tart flavor. Peas Farm, one of the vendors at my local farmers' market, always has a wide selection of vegetables, and it is the only vendor that carries fresh tomatillos. Their vibrant green skins peeking out from under wrinkly, papery husks always call to me. They make an excellent salsa when combined with the right ingredients. A tomatillo salsa isn't usually as sweet as a regular tomato salsa, but its lighter, more refreshing taste is great on a warm day served atop a finished dish or used in the cooking of a dish.

- 1 pound tomatillos
- 2 cloves garlic, left in skins
- ½ white onion
- 1 jalapeño, stemmed and seeded
- juice of 1 lime
- ⅓ cup fresh cilantro
- ½ teaspoon salt

1. Preheat the broiler to high and line a baking sheet with aluminum foil.

2. Remove the papery skins from the tomatillos and thoroughly wash the tomatillos to remove the waxy skins. Cut the tomatillos in half and place them cut side down on the foil-lined baking sheet, along with the garlic cloves. Broil for 5–6 minutes or until the skins start to char, flipping the garlic cloves halfway through cooking. Remove from the oven immediately.

3. Place the charred tomatillos and garlic cloves in a bowl covered with foil and let cool for 10 minutes. Once the tomatillos are cool enough to handle, remove the charred skins of both the tomatillos and the garlic cloves.

4. Place everything, including the juices from the bowl in which you placed the charred tomatillos, in a blender and purée until completely smooth.

Note: You can control the spiciness of this salsa by leaving in some of the jalapeño seeds. The more seeds you leave in, the spicier your salsa will be.

onion puree gravy

makes about 1¼ cups

This thick and hearty gravy goes great with any meal. My recipe is a surefire way to prove that you can make a rich and warming gravy without using flour. Slowly braising the onions in chicken stock makes them incredibly tender, perfect for puréeing into a smooth and velvety gravy. With its simple flavor tone, this gravy can be used for any type of meat or side dish. I'm pretty sure that any gravy-loving Southerner would gladly accept it—and probably would come back for another slathering.

- 2 tablespoons butter or ghee
- 1 medium yellow onion, coarsely chopped
- 2 cloves garlic, minced
- 1½ teaspoons tomato paste
- ½ cup chicken Mother Stock (page 144)
- salt and pepper to taste

1. In a medium-sized saucepan, heat the butter or ghee over medium heat. Add the onion and garlic and cook for 4 minutes, stirring occasionally, until the onions are softened. Add the tomato paste and stir to thoroughly incorporate, then pour in the stock while scraping the bottom of the pan with a wooden spoon. Season generously with salt and pepper and bring to a light simmer, then reduce the heat to low, cover, and simmer lightly for 15–20 minutes or until the onions are very tender.

2. Place everything in a blender or food processor and process until smooth.

nut butter

Nut butter is simple to make: All you do is grind up any type of nut until you get a nice runny, buttery consistency. By producing your own nut butters, you save money and have fresh-ground nut butter at your disposal. Make sure to use raw, not roasted, nuts.

- 2 cups raw nuts (almonds, cashews, hazelnuts, etc.)

1. Place the nuts in a food processor or blender and process until completely smooth, stopping to scrape the sides occasionally. Processing can take anywhere from 5—20 minutes, depending on how powerful your food processor or blender is. It may seem like it's taking a long time, but just keep processing and scraping until it turns into nut butter.

2. This nut butter can be stored in an airtight container at room temperature for 2—3 weeks or in the fridge for a couple of months.

Note: Prior to making nut butter, you can toast the nuts on a baking sheet lined with parchment paper in a 375°F oven for 12—15 minutes, shaking the baking sheet a few times to prevent burning.

chocolate roasted-hazelnut butter

You can't have just one universal nut butter recipe that is made with just nuts—sometimes you need a little variety. The best part about making this Chocolate Roasted-Hazelnut Butter—a "homemade Nutella," so to speak—is the aroma that fills the oven as the hazelnuts roast. I have a habit of leaning in as close to them as possible, to the point where I can hear each little nut crackling from the heat, so I can get a good whiff of the slightly sweet and nutty scent.

- 2 cups raw hazelnuts
- 2½ tablespoons unsweetened cacao powder
- 20 drops liquid stevia or 2 tablespoons coconut palm sugar
- ½ teaspoon pure vanilla extract

1. Preheat the oven to 375°F and line a baking sheet with parchment paper.

2. Spread the hazelnuts on the parchment-lined baking sheet and roast for 12—15 minutes, shaking the pan occasionally, until the nuts begin to brown and the skins begin to flake off easily. Place the roasted hazelnuts in a kitchen towel and rub them vigorously to remove the skins.

3. Transfer the hazelnuts to a food processor or blender and process until completely smooth and creamy. Add the cacao powder, stevia or coconut palm sugar, and vanilla and pulse a few times to incorporate, then process to blend completely.

4. This nut butter can be stored in an airtight container at room temperature for 2—3 weeks or in the fridge for a couple of months.

—— with gratitude ——

I have mentioned many times the dedication my parents gave to me. They have singlehandedly kept me moving strong my whole life. Mom and Dad, you kept me breathing when it was hard to breathe. If something brought me to my knees, you stood me back up. Everything I have achieved up to this point, from losing all that weight to writing this book, would have never been possible if it weren't for your boundless belief in me. No matter what it is that I want to do, you two always support me to the fullest without question. I'm often told by readers and fans of my blog that you guys must be so proud of me, and I know you are, but really it's me who's proud to have parents like you. People need to realize that regardless of what I've done, success would never have been possible without your ridiculous amounts of praise and support. I love the both of you more than anything in the entire spectrum of the universe, even though I may not always show it when I wake up in the morning. (Those morning grumbles are grumbles of love.) Thank you for always being there no matter what the circumstances.

Nick, I wish I was able to see you more often. Even though we don't have much time to get together, it's one of the things I look most forward to each year because we always have the best time. You and your gorgeous wife, Julia, always have something amazing planned for me when I come to New York, and you two always bring an impressive appetite to match mine. All the support and optimism you put forth during the writing of this book made it so much less stressful for me and actually made it seem doable. With your busy schedule and life, you still managed to set aside time to help me, which ended up making several things happen that might not have happened if you hadn't helped. You're one of the most influential people in my life, and I will always look up to you. Thanks for always being there. I love you and your awesome wife.

Jason and Lynsey, you two were among the biggest saviors in the making of this book, helping me get the cuts of meat I needed right when I needed them and filling my mind with wisdom. You supported me with love and kindness and pushed me in all the right directions when needed. Your constant optimism and belief in me, even when I was somewhat of a stranger to you, kept me going during difficult times and points of doubt. I cherish our friendship and consider you and your family a part of mine. Thank you so much for being the ones I can be weird with and talk about meat processing and kombucha with, and above all, thank you for feeding my family. I have so much respect for what you guys do, and I feel lucky to have people in my life like you two and your wild kids.

A lot of my attractions to less-common ethnic foods and my strange curiosity about foods that are out of the ordinary stem from you, Chachi, mainly because you were one of the few who exposed me to the real world through all those trips downtown and to the local hole-in-the-wall taco and papusa joints, all of which were absolutely delicious. I will never forget each and every one of those trips. Thank you for nurturing me as a child with love and food. Even though we are not blood related, you were always so motherly toward me and taught me things about real life that I couldn't have learned anywhere else. You were never just my nanny, but you are always my Chachi, and I love you.

Aunt Kathy, Jennifer, Caroline, and Uncle Larry, the photos in this book wouldn't be the same without your charitable contributions and never-ending time spent in antique shops around Texas. The fact that you were so willing to give up your time to bring me props, not knowing whether I would use them, means the world to me. It's not even funny how much time you saved me by helping with that. I am so grateful to have such supportive aunts, cousins, and uncles—thank y'all so much. See, you even got me saying y'all now.

Sharon Bowers, thank you for the push to make this book happen. Almost all my knowledge of book writing is because of you. I had no intention of writing a book, nor did I think I was even capable of writing a book, until you showed me that it was a strong possibility. Funny how a simple email flourished into one of the biggest accomplishments of my life so far.

Of course, thank you, Erich, Michele, Pam, and Susan for dealing with my endless questions at every turn in the making of this book. You always knew what to say to make me feel better when I had a question that seemed to have no answer. I truly appreciate the optimism and investment that you guys put forth in this book despite the fact that I'm so young.

A huge thank you to the book design team, because you guys spent a great deal of time on the illustrations at my ridiculous request. I had no idea that this much effort would be put into my book, and the fact that each illustration in here was hand-drawn completely humbles and blows me away. Not to mention that each of them looks absolutely stunning and turned out exactly how I imagined.

Last but not least, many thanks to all my friends in the food-blogging community who support what I do. Even though most of us know one another only through computer screens, I have made many real-life friends through this community in food, and that is an incredibly powerful thing that will stay with me for the rest of my life. I desperately wish I could list all of you, but there are too many names to add; you know who you are.

sources

Cooking with real, whole foods is easy and fun, but if you can't find some of the ingredients used in this book's recipes, here is a list of sources that I trust and use.

—— Grass-fed and pastured meats, poultry, eggs, and dairy ——

Yonder Way Farm
My local, go-to source for grass-fed and pastured meats, eggs, and dairy
(866) 577-2589
www.yonderwayfarm.com

The Barry Farm
Pastured turkey, pork, and lamb
thebarryfarm.com

Lava Lake Lamb
Grass-fed lamb
(888) 528-5253
www.lavalakelamb.com

US Wellness Meats
Grass-fed and pastured meats
(877) 383-0051
www.uswellnessmeats.com

Dreaming Cow
Grass-fed yogurt available at grocery store chains such as Central Market, Sprouts, and Whole Foods
(go to the website to locate a store near you)
www.dreamingcow.com

Maple Hill Creamery
Grass-fed organic yogurt available at grocery store chains such as Central Market, Sprouts, and Whole Foods (go to the website to locate a store near you)
www.maplehillcreamery.com

Cooking fats

Fatworks

Grass-fed tallow, pastured lard and duck fat

www.fatworksfoods.com

Kerrygold

Grass-fed butter and cheeses available at grocery stores

kerrygoldusa.com

La Tourangelle

Avocado oil and specialty oils

(866) NUT-OILS

latourangelle.com

Pure Indian Foods

Grass-fed organic ghee

www.pureindianfoods.com

Smjör Butter

Grass-fed butter available at grocery stores

www.smjor.is

Other ingredients

Bob's Red Mill

Coconut flour and arrowroot starch

(800) 349-2173

www.bobsredmill.com

Chameleon Cold Brew

Organic cold-brew coffee available at grocery store chains such as Whole Foods

www.chameleoncoldbrew.com

Coconut Secret

Coconut aminos

(888) 369-3393

www.coconutsecret.com

Honeyville

Blanched almond flour

(888) 810-3212

www.honeyville.com

Kasandrinos

Extra-virgin olive oil

www.kasandrinos.com

Navitas Naturals

Cacao powder, coconut sugar, and other organic ingredients

(888) 645-4282

navitasnaturals.com

Red Boat Fish Sauce

High-quality fish sauce

www.redboatfishsauce.com

Sweetleaf

Liquid stevia drops available at most grocery stores

(800) 899-9908

www.sweetleaf.com

Kitchen tools

Le Creuset

Cookware, bakeware, and kitchen utensils

(877) 418-5547

www.lecreuset.com

Fagor

Pressure cookers and kitchen gadgets

(800) 207-0806

www.fagoramerica.com

index